everyday
thai

Bath New York Singapore Hong Kong Cologne Delhi Melbourne

This edition published by parragon in 2008

Parragon Publishing
Queen Street House
4 Queen Street
Bath BA1 1HE, UK

ISBN 978-1-4075-3025-3

Printed in China

This book uses imperial, metric, and US cup measurements. Follow the same units of measurement throughout; do not mix imperial and metric. All spoon measurements are level, unless otherwise stated: teaspoons are assumed to be 5ml, and tablespoons are assumed to be 15ml. Unless otherwise stated, milk is assumed to be whole, eggs and individual fruits such as bananas are medium, and pepper is freshly ground black pepper.

Recipes using raw or very lightly cooked eggs should be avoided by infants, the elderly, pregnant women, convalescents, and anyone suffering from an illness. Pregnant and breast-feeding women are advised to avoid eating peanuts and peanut products.

everyday
thai

introduction

Thai cuisine has become increasingly popular in recent years, and with good reason – it's healthy, it's easy to prepare and cook, and it's very distinctive in its ingredients and flavors, making a Thai meal the perfect choice for any occasion from a quick midweek supper to an elegant themed dinner party for friends.

The main problem with cooking Thai-style used to be finding the ingredients, but because we have all become so much more ambitious in the kitchen, both supermarkets and smaller specialists stores have responded and now staples such as noodles and scented Thai rice, and flavorings such as the various curry pastes,

lemongrass, chilies, galangal, and coconut milk, are readily available. There are really no substitutes for these, so do make an effort to track them down – the internet is a good source of suppliers. Two exceptions

are palm sugar, which is less sweet than cane or beet sugar, and can be replaced with soft, light brown sugar or Indian "jaggery," and the aniseed-flavored Thai basil leaves, which can be replaced with common basil if you are unable to find them.

An essential piece of equipment in Thai cookery is the wok, which the Thai people use for everything – curries and soups, stir-fries and noodles, even deep-frying. A new steel wok needs seasoning before use, so wash it in warm, soapy water, scrubbing off the protective oiled coating, then rinse well and half dry. Stand the damp wok over low heat until it is completely dry, then drizzle in a little oil and wipe it around the inside of the wok with paper

towels. Continue to heat gently until the oil smokes and burns off, then repeat with another coating of oil. After this, the wok should never be scrubbed again, simply wiped out carefully.

Remember that every Thai meal is a relaxed and sociable event, and enjoy!

appetizers, soups & salads

This chapter is full of delicious ways to set the taste buds tingling at the start of a Thai meal. This is a concession to the Western custom of serving a separate first course, however – in Thailand, these dishes would be eaten either as snacks at any time during the day, or as appetizers before sitting down to a formal meal, or as part of the one main course, when small portions of several dishes are served on plates or in bowls and eaten together. A spoon and fork are used if, for example, a dish has a soupy consistency and includes rice or noodes, but often warm finger foods are also served which are picked up and dunked into a dipping sauce.

If you are planning to serve an authentic Thai menu, it is worth noting that soups feature in almost every Thai meal, even breakfast. Lunch is often a generous bowl of soup, a thin broth made filling and nutritious with the addition of rice or fine noodles, eggs, fish, meat, or tofu, vegetables and herbs, and a fresh chili or two.

When cooking deep-fried foods, remember to pat them well with paper towels when you remove them from the pan to absorb any excess oil and allow the delicate flavors of the filling to be enjoyed. And serve them lukewarm, Thai-style – not only will they taste perfect, but there will be no danger of scalded mouths.

omelet rolls

ingredients

SERVES 4

4 large eggs

2 tbsp. water

1 tbsp. Thai soy sauce

6 scallions, chopped finely

1 fresh red chili, seeded and
    chopped finely

1 tbsp. vegetable or
    peanut oil

1 tbsp. Thai green curry paste

bunch of fresh cilantro,
    chopped

method

Put the eggs, water, and Thai soy sauce in a bowl.
Set aside. Mix together the scallions and chopped chili
to form a paste.

Heat half the oil in an 8-inch skillet and pour in half
the egg mixture. Tilt to coat the bottom of the skillet
evenly and cook until set. Lift out and set aside. Heat
the remaining oil and make a second omelet in the
same way.

Spread the scallion and chili paste and the curry paste
in a thin layer over each omelet and sprinkle the cilantro
on top. Roll up tightly. Cut each one in half and then cut
each piece on the diagonal in half again. Serve
immediately, while still warm.

corn fritters

ingredients

SERVES 4

for the fritters

3 scallions, chopped finely

11 1/2 oz/325 g canned corn
    kernels, drained

1 red bell pepper, seeded and
    finely chopped

small handful of fresh
    cilantro, chopped

2 garlic cloves, crushed

2 eggs

2 tsp. superfine sugar

1 tbsp. fish sauce

2 tbsp. rice flour or cornstarch

vegetable or peanut oil,
    for pan-frying

for the dip

2 red bell peppers, seeded
    and halved

2 tomatoes, peeled, seeded,
    and chopped coarsely

1 tbsp. vegetable or peanut oil,
    for pan-frying

1 onion, chopped

1 tbsp. Thai red curry paste

3–4 sprigs fresh cilantro,
    chopped

method

Combine all the ingredients for the fritters in a bowl. Heat the oil in a skillet and cook spoonfuls of the mixture, in batches, until golden brown on the underside. Flip over with a spatula to cook the second side. Remove from the skillet, drain on paper towels, and keep warm.

To make the dip, put the red bell peppers on a baking sheet and place, skin-side up, under a hot broiler, until blackened. Using tongs, transfer to a plastic bag, tie the top, and let cool slightly.

When the bell peppers are cool enough to handle, peel off the skins and chop the flesh. Put into a blender or food processor with the tomatoes and process until smooth.

Heat the oil in a heavy-bottom pan and cook the onion and curry paste for 3–4 minutes, until softened. Add the bell pepper and tomato purée and cook gently until tender and hot. Stir in the chopped cilantro, cook for 1 minute, and serve hot with the fritters.

wontons

ingredients

SERVES 4

for the filling

2 tbsp. vegetable or peanut oil

6 scallions, chopped

4¹/₂ oz/125 g mushrooms,
  chopped

2 oz/55 g fine green beans,
  chopped

2 oz/55 g corn kernels,
  drained if canned

1 egg, beaten

3 tbsp. Thai soy sauce

1 tbsp. jaggery or soft light
  brown sugar

¹/₂ tsp. salt

for the wontons

24 wonton skins

1 egg, beaten

vegetable or peanut oil,
  for deep-frying

plum or chili sauce, to serve

method

To make the filling, heat the oil in a preheated wok and stir-fry the scallions, mushrooms, and beans for 1–2 minutes, until softened. Add the corn, stir well to mix, and then push the vegetables to the side. Pour in the egg. Stir until lightly set before incorporating the vegetables and adding the soy sauce, sugar, and salt. Remove the wok from the heat.

Place the wonton skins in a pile on a counter. Put a teaspoonful of the filling in the center of the top skin. Brush the edges with beaten egg and fold in half diagonally to make a small triangular package. Repeat with the remaining skins and filling.

Heat the oil for deep-frying in a wok or large skillet. Add the packages, in batches, and deep-fry for 3–4 minutes, until they are golden brown. Remove from the wok with a slotted spoon and drain on paper towels. Keep warm while you cook the remaining wontons. Serve hot with plum or chili sauce.

crispy egg rolls

ingredients

SERVES 4

2 tbsp. vegetable or peanut oil

6 scallions, cut into 2-inch
    lengths

1 fresh green chili, seeded
    and chopped

1 carrot, cut into thin sticks

1 zucchini, cut into thin sticks

1/2 red bell pepper, seeded
    and thinly sliced

4 oz/115 g/3/4 cup bean
    sprouts

4 oz/115 g canned bamboo
    shoots, drained and rinsed

3 tbsp. Thai soy sauce

1–2 tbsp. chili sauce

8 egg roll skins

vegetable or peanut oil,
    for deep-frying

method

Heat the oil in a wok and stir-fry the scallions and chili
for 30 seconds. Add the carrot, zucchini, and red bell
pepper and stir-fry for 1 minute more. Remove the wok
from heat and stir in the bean sprouts, bamboo shoots,
soy sauce, and chili sauce. Taste and add more soy
sauce or chili sauce if necessary.

Place an egg roll skin on a counter and spoon some of
the vegetable mixture diagonally across the center. Roll
one corner over the filling and flip the sides of the skin
over the top to enclose the filling. Continue to roll up to
make an enclosed package. Repeat with the remaining
skins and filling to make 8 egg rolls.

Heat the oil for deep-frying in a wok or large skillet.
Deep-fry the egg rolls, 3–4 at a time, until they are crisp
and golden brown. Remove with a slotted spoon, drain
on paper towels while you cook the remainder, then
serve immediately.

lemongrass chicken skewers

ingredients

SERVES 4

2 long or 4 short lemongrass
    stems
2 large skinless, boneless
    chicken breasts, about
    14 oz/400 g in total
1 small egg white
1 carrot, finely grated
1 small fresh red chili, seeded
    and chopped
2 tbsp. snipped fresh garlic
    chives
2 tbsp. chopped cilantro
salt and pepper
1 tbsp. corn oil

to garnish

cilantro sprigs
lime slices
mixed salad greens, to serve

method

If the lemongrass stems are long, cut them in half across
the center to make 4 short lengths. Cut each stem in half
lengthwise, so that you have 8 sticks.

Coarsely chop the chicken pieces and place them in a
food processor with the egg white. Process to a smooth
paste, then add the carrot, chili, chives, cilantro, and
salt and pepper to taste. Process for a few seconds to
mix well. Transfer the mixture to a large bowl. Cover and
chill in the refrigerator for 15 minutes.

Preheat the broiler to medium. Divide the mixture into
8 equal-size portions and use your hands to shape the
mixture around the lemongrass "skewers."

Brush the skewers with oil and cook under the hot broiler
for 4–6 minutes, turning them occasionally, until golden
brown and thoroughly cooked. Alternatively, grill over
medium–hot coals.

Transfer to serving plates. Garnish with cilantro sprigs
and lime slices and serve hot with salad greens.

chicken satay

ingredients

SERVES 4

2 tbsp. vegetable or peanut oil
1 tbsp. sesame oil
juice of 1/2 lime
2 skinless, boneless chicken
    breasts, cut into small
    cubes

for the dip

2 tbsp. vegetable or peanut oil
1 small onion, chopped finely
1 small fresh green chili,
    seeded and chopped
1 garlic clove, chopped finely
4 fl oz/125 ml/1/2 cup crunchy
    peanut butter
6–8 tbsp. water
juice of 1/2 lime

method

Combine both the oils and the lime juice in a
nonmetallic dish. Add the chicken cubes, cover with
plastic wrap, and let chill for 1 hour.

To make the dip, heat the oil in a skillet and sauté the
onion, chili, and garlic over low heat, stirring occasionally,
for about 5 minutes, until just softened. Add the peanut
butter, water, and lime juice and let simmer gently, stirring
constantly, until the peanut butter has softened enough to
make a dip—you may need to add extra water to make a
thinner consistency.

Meanwhile, drain the chicken cubes and thread them
onto 8–12 wooden skewers – soak the skewers in cold
water for 45 minutes before threading the meat to help
stop them burning during cooking. Put under a hot
broiler or on a barbecue, turning frequently, for about
10 minutes, until cooked and browned. Serve hot with
the warm dip.

crispy wrapped shrimp

ingredients

SERVES 4

16 large, unpeeled cooked
    shrimp
juice of 1 lime
4 tbsp. chili sauce
16 wonton skins
vegetable or peanut oil,
    for deep-frying
plum sauce, to serve

method

Remove the heads and shell the shrimp, but leave the tails intact. Place them in a nonmetallic bowl, add the lime juice, and toss lightly to coat. Set aside in a cool place for 30 minutes.

Spread a little chili sauce over a wonton skin. Place a shrimp diagonally across it, leaving the tail protruding. Fold the bottom corner of the skin over the shrimp, fold the next corner up over the head end, and then roll the shrimp up in the skin so that the body is encased, but the tail is exposed. Repeat with the remaining skins, chili sauce, and shrimp.

Heat the oil in a wok or skillet and deep-fry the shrimp, in batches, until crisp and browned. Serve hot with plum sauce for dipping.

fish cakes

ingredients

SERVES 4

1 lb/450 g skinned white fish
    fillets, cut into cubes

1 egg white

2 kaffir lime leaves, torn
    coarsely

1 tbsp. Thai green curry paste

55 g/2 oz green beans,
    chopped finely

1 fresh red chili, seeded and
    chopped finely

bunch of fresh cilantro,
    chopped

vegetable or peanut oil for
    cooking

1 fresh red chili, seeded and
    sliced, to serve

for the dipping sauce

4 oz/115 g/generous $^1/_2$ cup
    superfine sugar

2 fl oz/50 ml/$^1/_4$ cup white
    wine vinegar

1 small carrot, cut into thin
    sticks

2-inch/5-cm piece cucumber,
    peeled, seeded, and cut
    into thin sticks

method

Put the fish into a food processor with the egg white,
lime leaves, and curry paste, and process until smooth.
Scrape the mixture into a bowl and stir in the green
beans, red chili, and cilantro.

With dampened hands, shape the mixture into small
patties, about 2 inches across. Place them on a large
plate in a single layer and let chill for 30 minutes.

Meanwhile, make the dipping sauce. Put the sugar in
a pan with $1^1/_2$ tablespoons water and the vinegar and
heat gently, stirring until the sugar has dissolved. Add
the carrot and cucumber, then remove from the heat
and let cool.

Heat the oil in a skillet and cook the fish cakes, in batches,
until golden brown on both sides. Drain on paper towels
and keep warm while you cook the remaining batches.
If desired, reheat the dipping sauce. Serve the fish cakes
immediately with warm or cold dipping sauce, topped with
the red chili slices.

beef satay with peanut sauce

ingredients

SERVES 4

1 lb 2 oz/500 g lean beef fillet

2 garlic cloves, crushed

3/4-inch/2-cm piece fresh
    gingerroot, finely grated

1 tbsp. brown sugar

1 tbsp. dark soy sauce

1 tbsp. lime juice

2 tsp. sesame oil

1 tsp. ground coriander

1 tsp. ground turmeric

1/2 tsp. chili powder

peanut sauce

10 fl oz/280 ml/1 1/4 cups
    coconut milk

8 tbsp. chunky peanut butter

1/2 small onion, grated

2 tsp. brown sugar

1/2 tsp. chili powder

1 tbsp. dark soy sauce

to garnish

chopped cucumber

red bell pepper pieces

method

Cut the beef into 1/2-inch/1-cm cubes and place in a large bowl.

Add the garlic, ginger, sugar, soy sauce, lime juice, sesame oil, coriander, turmeric, and chili powder. Mix well to coat the pieces of meat evenly. Cover and let marinate in the refrigerator for at least 2 hours or overnight.

Preheat the broiler to high. To make the peanut sauce, place all the ingredients in a small pan and stir over medium heat until boiling. Remove the pan from the heat and keep warm.

Thread the beef cubes on to presoaked bamboo skewers. Cook the skewers under the hot broiler for 3–5 minutes, turning frequently, until golden. Alternatively, grill over hot coals. Transfer to a large serving plate, then garnish with chopped cucumber and red bell pepper pieces and serve with the peanut sauce.

pork & crab meatballs

ingredients

SERVES 6

8 oz/225 g pork fillet,
    chopped finely
5¾ oz/170 g canned
    crabmeat, drained
3 scallions, chopped finely
1 garlic clove, chopped finely
1 tsp. Thai red curry paste
1 tbsp. cornstarch
1 egg white
vegetable or peanut oil,
    for deep-frying
boiled rice, to serve

for the sauce

1 tbsp. vegetable or peanut oil
2 shallots, chopped
1 garlic clove, crushed
2 large fresh red chilies,
    seeded and chopped
4 scallions, chopped
3 tomatoes, chopped coarsely

method

Put the pork and crabmeat into a bowl and mix together.
Add the scallions, garlic, curry paste, cornstarch, and
egg white, and beat well to make a thick paste. With
damp hands shape the mixture into walnut-size balls.

Heat the oil in a wok and deep-fry the balls, in batches,
for 3–4 minutes, turning frequently, until golden brown
and cooked. Drain on paper towels and keep warm.

To make the sauce, heat the oil in a wok and stir-fry
the shallots and garlic for 1–2 minutes. Add the chilies
and scallions and stir-fry for 1–2 minutes, then add the
tomatoes. Stir together quickly, then spoon the sauce over
the pork and crab balls. Serve immediately with rice.

vegetable &
noodle soup

ingredients

SERVES 4

2 tbsp. vegetable or peanut oil

1 onion, sliced

2 garlic cloves, chopped finely

1 large carrot, cut into thin sticks

1 zucchini, cut into thin sticks

4 oz/115 g broccoli, cut into
    florets

$1^3/4$ pints/1 litre/4 cups
    vegetable stock

14 fl oz/400 ml/$1^3/4$ cups
    coconut milk

3–4 tbsp. Thai soy sauce

2 tbsp. Thai red curry paste

2 oz/55 g wide rice noodles

4 oz/115 g/$^3/4$ cup mung or
    soy bean sprouts

4 tbsp. chopped fresh cilantro

method

Heat the oil in a wok or large skillet and stir-fry the onion
and garlic for 2–3 minutes. Add the carrot, zucchini, and
broccoli and stir-fry for 3–4 minutes, until just tender.

Pour in the stock and coconut milk and bring to a boil. Add
the soy sauce, curry paste, and noodles, and let simmer
for 2–3 minutes, until the noodles have swelled. Stir in
the bean sprouts and cilantro and serve immediately.

shrimp laksa

ingredients

SERVES 4

14 oz/400 g/1¾ cups canned
    coconut milk

10 fl oz/280 ml/1¼ cups
    vegetable stock

1¾ oz/50 g vermicelli rice
    noodles

1 red bell pepper, seeded and
    cut into strips

8 oz/225 g canned bamboo
    shoots, drained and rinsed

2-inch/5-cm piece fresh
    ginger, sliced thinly

3 scallions, chopped

1 tbsp. Thai red curry paste

2 tbsp. fish sauce

1 tsp. jaggery or soft light
    brown sugar

6 sprigs fresh Thai basil

12 unshelled cooked shrimp

method

Pour the coconut milk and stock into a pan and bring
slowly to a boil. Add the remaining ingredients, except
the shrimp, and let simmer gently for 4–5 minutes,
until the noodles are cooked.

Add the shrimp and let simmer for an additional
1–2 minutes, until heated through. Ladle the soup
into small, warmed bowls, dividing the shrimp equally
between them, and serve.

corn & crab soup

ingredients

SERVES 4

2 tbsp. vegetable or peanut oil

4 garlic cloves, chopped finely

5 shallots, chopped finely

2 lemongrass stalks, chopped finely

1-inch/2.5-cm piece fresh ginger, chopped finely

1³/₄ pints/1 litre/4 cups chicken stock

14 oz/400 g/1³/₄ cups canned coconut milk

8 oz/225 g/scant 1¹/₂ cups frozen corn kernels

12 oz/350 g canned crabmeat, drained and shredded

2 tbsp. fish sauce

juice of 1 lime

1 tsp. jaggery or soft light brown sugar

bunch of fresh cilantro, chopped, to garnish

method

Heat the oil in a large skillet and sauté the garlic, shallots, lemongrass, and ginger over low heat, stirring occasionally, for 2–3 minutes, until softened. Add the stock and coconut milk and bring to a boil. Add the corn, reduce the heat, and let simmer gently for 3–4 minutes.

Add the crabmeat, fish sauce, lime juice, and sugar, and let simmer gently for 1 minute. Ladle into warmed bowls, garnish with the chopped cilantro, and serve immediately.

spicy beef &
noodle soup

ingredients

SERVES 4

1³/4 pints/1 litre/4 cups beef
    stock

¹/4 pint/150 ml/²/3 cup
    vegetable or peanut oil

3 oz/85 g rice vermicelli
    noodles

2 shallots, sliced thinly

2 garlic cloves, crushed

1-inch/2.5-cm piece fresh
    ginger, sliced thinly

8-oz/225-g piece fillet steak,
    cut into thin strips

2 tbsp. Thai green curry paste

2 tbsp. Thai soy sauce

1 tbsp. fish sauce

chopped fresh cilantro,
    to garnish

method

Pour the stock into a large pan and bring to a boil.
Meanwhile, heat the oil in a wok or large skillet. Add a
third of the noodles and cook for 10–20 seconds, until
they have puffed up. Lift out of the oil with tongs,
drain on paper towels, and set aside. Discard all but
2 tablespoons of the oil.

Add the shallots, garlic, and ginger to the wok or skillet
and stir-fry for 1 minute. Add the beef and curry paste
and stir-fry for an additional 3–4 minutes, until tender.

Add the beef mixture, the uncooked noodles, soy sauce,
and fish sauce to the pan of stock and let simmer for
2–3 minutes, until the noodles have swelled. Serve hot,
garnished with the chopped cilantro and the reserved
crispy noodles.

rice noodles with tofu soup

ingredients

SERVES 4

7 oz/200 g firm tofu, drained

vegetable or peanut oil,
    for deep-frying

1³/₄ pints/1 litre/4 cups
    vegetable stock

5 scallions, halved

1 yellow bell pepper, seeded
    and sliced

2 celery stalks, sliced

1 small onion, sliced thinly

4 kaffir lime leaves

2 tbsp. Thai soy sauce

1 tbsp. Thai green curry paste

6 oz/175 g wide rice noodles,
    soaked and drained

chopped fresh cilantro,
    to garnish

method

Using a sharp knife, cut the tofu into even cubes. Pour
the oil into a wok to a depth of about 2 inches and heat.
Deep-fry the tofu, in batches, until browned all over.
Remove with a slotted spoon, drain on paper towels,
and set aside.

Pour the stock into a pan and bring to a boil. Add
the scallions, yellow bell pepper, celery, onion, lime
leaves, soy sauce, and curry paste, and let simmer for
4–5 minutes. Add the noodles and the tofu and let
simmer for 2–3 minutes. Ladle into warmed bowls and
serve hot, topped with chopped cilantro.

clear soup with mushrooms & chicken

ingredients

SERVES 4

1 oz/25 g/¹/₄ cup dried cèpes
    or other mushrooms

1³/₄ pints/1 litre/4 cups water

2 tbsp. vegetable or peanut oil

4 oz/115 g mushrooms,
    sliced

2 garlic cloves, chopped
    coarsely

2-inch/5-cm piece fresh
    galangal, sliced thinly

2 chicken breast portions
    (on the bone, skin on)

8 oz/225 g baby cremini or
    white mushrooms,
    quartered

juice of ¹/₂ lime

sprigs fresh flat-leaf parsley,
    to garnish

method

Place the dried mushrooms in a small bowl and pour over hot water to cover. Set aside to soak for 20–30 minutes. Drain the mushrooms, reserving the soaking liquid. Cut off and discard the stalks and chop the caps coarsely.

Pour the reserved soaking water into a pan with the measured water and bring to a boil. Reduce the heat to a simmer.

Meanwhile, heat the oil in a wok and stir-fry the soaked mushrooms, sliced fresh mushrooms, garlic, and galangal for 3–4 minutes. Add to the pan of hot water with the chicken breasts. Let simmer for 10–15 minutes, until the meat comes off the bones easily.

Remove the chicken from the pan. Peel off and set aside the skin. Remove the meat from the bones, slice, and set aside. Return the skin and bones to the stock and let simmer for an additional 30 minutes.

Remove the pan from the heat and strain the stock into a clean pan through a cheesecloth-lined strainer. Bring back to a boil and add the cremini or white mushrooms, sliced chicken, and lime juice. Reduce the heat and let simmer for 8-10 minutes. Ladle into warmed bowls, garnish with parsley sprigs, and serve immediately.

hot-and-sour soup

ingredients

SERVES 4

6 dried shiitake mushrooms

4 oz/115 g rice vermicelli
   noodles

4 small fresh green chilies,
   seeded and chopped

6 tbsp. rice wine vinegar

1$^{1}/_{2}$ pints/850 ml/3$^{1}/_{2}$ cups
   vegetable stock

2 lemongrass stalks, snapped
   in half

4 oz/115 g canned water
   chestnuts, drained, rinsed,
   and halved

6 tbsp. Thai soy sauce

juice of 1 lime

1 tbsp. jaggery or soft light
   brown sugar

3 scallions, chopped,
   to garnish

method

Place the dried mushrooms in a bowl and pour in
enough hot water to cover. Set aside to soak for 1 hour.
Place the noodles in another bowl and pour in enough
hot water to cover. Set aside to soak for 10 minutes.
Combine the chilies and rice wine vinegar in a third
bowl and set aside.

Drain the mushrooms and noodles. Bring the stock
to a boil in a large pan. Add the mushrooms, noodles,
lemongrass, water chestnuts, soy sauce, lime juice,
and sugar, and bring to a boil.

Stir in the chili and vinegar mixture and cook for
1–2 minutes. Remove and discard the lemon grass.
Ladle the soup into warmed bowls and serve hot,
garnished with the scallions.

peppered beef salad

ingredients

SERVES 4

4 4-oz/115-g fillet steaks

2 tbsp. black peppercorns, crushed

1 tsp. Chinese five spice powder

4 oz/115 g/³/₄ cup bean sprouts

1-inch/2.5 -m piece ginger, chopped finely

4 shallots, sliced finely

1 red bell pepper, seeded and sliced thinly

3 tbsp. Thai soy sauce

2 fresh red chilies, seeded and sliced

¹/₂ lemongrass stalk, chopped finely

3 tbsp. vegetable or peanut oil

1 tbsp. sesame oil

method

Wash the steaks and pat dry on paper towels. Mix the peppercorns with the five spice and press onto all sides of the steaks. Cook on a grill pan or under a broiler for 2–3 minutes each side, or until cooked to your liking.

Meanwhile mix the bean sprouts, half the ginger, the shallots, and bell pepper together and divide between 4 plates. Mix the remaining ginger, soy sauce, chilies, lemongrass, and oils together.

Slice the beef and arrange on the vegetables. Drizzle with the dressing and serve immediately.

shrimp &
papaya salad

ingredients

SERVES 4

1 papaya, peeled
12 oz/350 g large cooked
    shrimp, shelled

for the dressing

4 scallions, chopped finely
2 fresh red chilies, seeded
    and chopped finely
1 tsp. fish sauce
1 tbsp. vegetable or peanut oil
juice of 1 lime
1 tsp. jaggery or soft light
    brown sugar

assorted baby salad greens

method

Scoop the seeds out of the papaya and slice thinly. Stir gently together with the shrimp.

Mix the scallions, chilies, fish sauce, oil, lime juice, and sugar together.

Arrange the salad greens in a bowl and top with the papaya and shrimp. Pour the dressing over the salad and serve immediately.

crab & cilantro salad

ingredients

SERVES 4

12 oz/350 g canned white
    crabmeat, drained
4 scallions, finely chopped
handful of fresh cilantro,
    chopped

for the dressing

1 garlic clove, crushed
1-inch/2.5-cm piece ginger,
    peeled and grated
2 lime leaves, torn into pieces
juice of 1 lime
1 tsp. fish sauce

1 iceberg lettuce, shredded
3-inch/7.5-cm piece
    cucumber, chopped

method

Put the crabmeat into a bowl and stir in the scallions
and cilantro.

Mix the ingredients for the dressing together.

Place the lettuce leaves on a serving platter and sprinkle
with the cucumber.

Arrange the crab salad over the leaves and drizzle the
dressing over the salad. Serve immediately.

tuna & tomato salad with ginger dressing

ingredients

SERVES 4

$1/2$ cup shredded Napa
   cabbage

3 tbsp. rice wine or dry sherry

2 tbsp. Thai fish sauce

1 tbsp. finely shredded fresh
   gingerroot

1 garlic clove, finely chopped

$1/2$ small fresh red Thai chili,
   finely chopped

2 tsp. brown sugar

2 tbsp. lime juice

14 oz/400 g fresh tuna steak

corn oil, for brushing

$4^{1}/_{2}$ oz/125 g cherry tomatoes

fresh mint leaves and mint
   sprigs, coarsely chopped,
   to garnish

method

Place a small pile of shredded Napa cabbage on a large
serving plate. Place the rice wine or dry sherry, fish
sauce, ginger, garlic, chili, sugar, and 1 tablespoon of
lime juice in a screw-top jar and shake well to combine.

Using a sharp knife, cut the tuna into strips of an even
thickness. Sprinkle with the remaining lime juice.

Brush a wide skillet or ridged grill pan with oil and heat
until very hot. Arrange the tuna strips in the skillet and
cook until just firm and light golden, turning them over
once. Remove the tuna strips from the skillet and reserve.

Add the tomatoes to the skillet and cook over high heat
until lightly browned. Spoon the tuna and tomatoes over
the Napa cabbage, then spoon over the dressing.
Garnish with fresh mint and serve warm.

eggplant &
onion salad

ingredients

SERVES 4

4 tbsp. vegetable or peanut oil

1 onion, sliced

4 shallots, chopped finely

4 scallions, sliced

12 oz/350 g eggplants, cubed

2 tbsp. Thai green curry paste

2 tbsp. Thai soy sauce

1 tsp. jaggery or soft light
brown sugar

4 oz/115 g block creamed
coconut, chopped

3 tbsp. water

small handful of fresh cilantro,
chopped

few Thai basil leaves, chopped

small handful of fresh parsley,
chopped

4 oz/115 g/2^1/$_2$ cups arugula
leaves

2 tbsp. sweet chili sauce

method

Heat half the oil in a wok or large skillet and cook all the
onions together for 1–2 minutes, until just softened but
not browned. Lift out and set aside.

Cook the eggplant cubes, in batches if necessary, adding
more oil as needed, until they are crisp and golden brown.

Return the onions to the wok and add the curry paste,
soy sauce, and sugar. Add the creamed coconut and
water and cook until dissolved. Stir in most of the
cilantro, the basil, and the parsley.

Toss the arugula in the sweet chili sauce and serve
with the eggplant and onion salad. Garnish with the
remaining herbs.

hot-and-sour vegetable salad

ingredients

SERVES 4

2 tbsp. vegetable or peanut oil

1 tbsp. chili oil

1 onion, sliced

1-inch/2.5-cm piece ginger,
    grated

1 small head broccoli, cut
    into florets

2 carrots, cut into short thin
    sticks

1 red bell pepper, seeded and
    cut into squares

1 yellow bell pepper, seeded
    and cut into strips

2 oz/50 g snow peas,
    trimmed and halved

2 oz/50 g baby corn, halved

for the dressing

2 tbsp. vegetable or peanut oil

1 tsp. chili oil

1 tbsp. rice wine vinegar

juice of 1 lime

$^1/_2$ tsp. fish sauce

method

Heat the oils in a wok or large skillet and sauté the onion
and ginger for 1–2 minutes until they start to soften. Add
the vegetables and stir-fry for 2–3 minutes until they have
softened slightly. Remove from the heat and set aside.

Mix the dressing ingredients together. Transfer the
vegetables to a serving plate and drizzle the dressing
over. Serve warm immediately, or let the flavors develop
and serve cold.

curried egg salad

ingredients

SERVES 4

6 eggs

1 tbsp. vegetable or peanut oil

1 onion, chopped

1 tbsp. Thai yellow curry
paste

4 tbsp. plain yogurt

1/2 tsp. salt

handful of fresh cilantro,
chopped finely

bunch of watercress or
arugula

2 zucchinis, cut into short
thin sticks

1 fresh green chili, seeded
and chopped finely

1 tsp. fish sauce

1 tsp. rice wine vinegar

3 tbsp. vegetable or peanut oil

method

Put the eggs in a pan, cover with cold water, and bring
to a boil. Let simmer for 10 minutes, then drain and
rinse in cold water. Shell and halve.

Meanwhile, heat the oil in a medium skillet and sauté
the onion gently until softened but not browned. Remove
from the heat and stir in the curry paste. Let cool slightly
before stirring in the yogurt, salt, and half the cilantro.
Set the mixture aside.

Arrange the watercress and zucchinis on a platter. Mix
the chili, fish sauce, vinegar, and oil together and pour
the dressing over the leaves.

Arrange the eggs on top and spoon the yogurt mixture
over each one. Garnish with the remaining cilantro over
the top and serve immediately.

for meat lovers

The Thai Buddhist religion forbids the killing of animals, but – somewhat confusingly – not the eating of meat, which is supplied mainly by non-Buddhist butchers who are immigrants to Thailand, and is often regarded as a treat for special occasions.

Meat is cooked in a variety of ways – in curries and stir-fries, on skewers, or marinated and roasted – with wonderful seasonings that result in a dish that is hot, spicy, and irresistibly tasty. Beef, pork, and lamb are all served, but chicken is the most common, with duck another Thai favorite, frequently cooked under a broiler with warm spices and soy or sweet glazes. Both chicken and pork are often combined with seafood such as shrimp or crabmeat, and tossed with noodles, which – after rice – are Thailand's main staple. Pad Thai, a combination of rice noodles, pork, and shrimp, tossed together with garlic, chili, eggs, and peanuts, is the best known of all Thai noodle dishes and is the country's "fast-food" dish.

Thai meat dishes are quick and easy to cook – curries more or less take care of themselves once the initial preparation is complete, needing only some freshly cooked rice to serve, while stir-fries are prepared, cooked, and served literally in minutes, with meat, vegetables, and noodles all thrown in together.

spicy beef with potato

ingredients

SERVES 4

1 lb/450 g beef fillet

2 tbsp. Thai soy sauce

2 tbsp. fish sauce

2 tbsp. vegetable or peanut oil

3–4 cilantro roots, chopped

1 tbsp. crushed black
    peppercorns

2 garlic cloves, chopped

1 tbsp. jaggery or soft light
    brown sugar

12 oz/350 g potatoes, diced

$1/4$ pint/150 ml/$2/3$ cup water

bunch of scallions, chopped

8 oz/225 g/5 cups baby
    spinach leaves

cooked rice or noodles,
    to serve

method

Cut the beef into thick slices and place in a shallow dish. Put the soy sauce, fish sauce, 1 tablespoon of the oil, the cilantro roots, peppercorns, garlic, and sugar in a food processor and process to a thick paste. Scrape the paste into the dish and toss the beef to coat. Cover with plastic wrap and set aside to marinate in the refrigerator for at least 3 hours, preferably overnight.

Heat the remaining oil in a wok. Lift the beef out of the marinade, reserving the marinade, and cook for 3–4 minutes on each side, until browned. Add the reserved marinade and the potatoes with the measured water and gradually bring to a boil. Let simmer for 6–8 minutes, or until the potatoes are tender.

Add the scallions and spinach. Cook gently until the greens have wilted. Serve immediately with rice or noodles.

mussaman curry

ingredients

SERVES 4

1 tbsp. vegetable or peanut oil

1 lb/450 g beef top round, cut into cubes

2 tbsp. Mussaman curry paste

2 large onions, cut into wedges

2 large potatoes, cut into chunks

14 fl oz/400 ml/1³/₄ cups coconut milk

¹/₄ pint/150 ml/²/₃ cup water

2 cardamom pods

2 tbsp. tamarind paste

2 tsp. jaggery or soft light brown sugar

2³/₄ oz/75 g/²/₃ cup unsalted peanuts, toasted or dry-fried

1 fresh red chili, sliced thinly

boiled rice, to serve

method

Heat the oil in a wok and cook the meat, in batches, until browned all over. Remove with a slotted spoon and set aside.

Add the curry paste to the wok and stir-fry for 1–2 minutes. Add the onions and potatoes and stir-fry for 4–5 minutes, until golden brown. Remove with a slotted spoon and set aside.

Pour the coconut milk into the wok with the measured water and bring to a boil. Reduce the heat and let simmer for 8–10 minutes.

Return the meat and cooked vegetables to the wok. Add the cardamom, tamarind paste, and sugar, and let simmer for 15–20 minutes, until the meat is tender. Stir in the peanuts and chili and serve with rice.

hot beef & coconut curry

ingredients

SERVES 4

14 fl oz/400 ml//1 ¾ cups
    coconut milk

2 tbsp. Thai red curry paste

2 garlic cloves, crushed

1 lb 2 oz/500 g braising steak

2 fresh kaffir lime leaves,
    shredded

3 tbsp. lime juice

2 tbsp. Thai fish sauce

1 large fresh red chili, seeded
    and sliced

½ tsp. ground turmeric

salt and pepper

2 tbsp. chopped fresh basil
    leaves

2 tbsp. chopped cilantro
    leaves

shredded coconut, to garnish

freshly cooked rice, to serve

method

Place the coconut milk in a large pan and bring to a boil. Reduce the heat and simmer gently for 10 minutes, or until it has thickened. Stir in the curry paste and garlic and simmer for an additional 5 minutes.

Cut the beef into ¾-inch/2-cm chunks. Add to the pan and bring to a boil, stirring constantly. Reduce the heat and add the kaffir lime leaves, lime juice, fish sauce, sliced chili, turmeric, and ½ teaspoon of salt.

Cover the pan and continue simmering for 20–25 minutes, or until the meat is tender, adding a little water if the sauce looks too dry.

Stir in the basil and cilantro and season to taste with salt and pepper. Sprinkle with shredded coconut and serve with freshly cooked rice.

beef stir-fry

ingredients

SERVES 4

2 tbsp. vegetable or peanut oil

2 medium red onions,
    sliced thinly

2 garlic cloves, chopped

1-inch/2.5-cm piece ginger,
    cut into thin sticks

2 4-oz/115 g beef fillets, sliced
    thinly

1 green bell pepper, seeded
    and sliced

150 g/5$^1/_2$ oz canned bamboo
    shoots

4 oz/115 g/$^3/_4$ cup bean
    sprouts

2 tbsp. magic paste

1 tbsp. Thai red curry paste

handful of fresh cilantro,
    chopped

few sprigs Thai basil

boiled rice, to serve

method

Heat the oil in a wok or large skillet and stir-fry the
onions, garlic, and ginger for 1 minute. Add the beef
strips and stir-fry over high heat until browned all over.
Add the vegetables and the two pastes and cook for
2–3 minutes until blended and cooked.

Stir in the cilantro and basil and serve immediately
with boiled rice.

coconut beef curry

ingredients

SERVES 4

1 tbsp. ground coriander

1 tbsp. ground cumin

3 tbsp. Mussaman curry paste

$^1/_4$ pint/150 ml/$^2/_3$ cup water

2$^3/_4$ oz/75 g block creamed
    coconut

1 lb/450 g beef fillet, cut into
    strips

14 fl oz/400 ml/1$^3/_4$ cups
    coconut milk

1$^3/_4$ oz/50 g/$^1/_2$ cup unsalted
    peanuts, chopped finely

2 tbsp. fish sauce

1 tsp. soft light brown sugar

4 kaffir lime leaves

boiled rice and chopped fresh
    cilantro, to serve

method

Combine the coriander, cumin, and curry paste in a
bowl. Pour the measured water into a pan, add the
creamed coconut, and heat until it has dissolved. Add
the curry paste mixture and let simmer for 1 minute.

Add the beef and let simmer for 6–8 minutes, then add
the coconut milk, peanuts, fish sauce, and sugar. Let
simmer gently for 15–20 minutes, until the meat is tender.

Add the lime leaves and let simmer for 1–2 minutes.
Serve the curry hot with boiled rice with chopped fresh
cilantro stirred through it.

beef with fresh noodles

ingredients

SERVES 4

6 dried black cloud Chinese
    mushrooms

2 tbsp. vegetable or peanut oil

2 8-oz/225 g sirloin steaks,
    sliced thickly

1 onion, cut into thin wedges

2 garlic cloves, chopped

1 green bell pepper, seeded
    and chopped

3 celery stalks, sliced

2 tbsp. Thai green curry paste

1/2 pint/300 ml/1 1/4 cups beef
    stock

4 tbsp. black bean sauce

8 oz/225 g fresh egg noodles

4 tbsp. chopped fresh parsley

method

Put the mushrooms in a bowl, cover with boiling water,
and set aside to soak for 30 minutes. Drain. Break up
any larger pieces.

Heat the oil in a wok and stir-fry the steak over high heat
until browned. Add the mushrooms, onion, garlic, bell
pepper, and celery, and stir-fry for 3–4 minutes. Add the
curry paste, beef stock, and black bean sauce, and stir-fry
for 2–3 minutes.

Meanwhile, cook the noodles in boiling water for 3–4 minutes,
drain well, and stir into the wok. Sprinkle the parsley over and
stir. Serve immediately.

red-hot beef
with cashew nuts

ingredients

SERVES 4

1 lb 2 oz/500 g lean boneless
    beef sirloin
1 tsp. vegetable oil

marinade

1 tbsp. sesame seeds
1 garlic clove, chopped
1 tbsp. finely chopped fresh
    gingerroot
1 fresh red Thai chili, chopped
2 tbsp. dark soy sauce
1 tsp. Thai red curry paste

to finish

1 tsp. sesame oil
4 tbsp. unsalted cashew nuts
1 scallion, thickly sliced
    diagonally
cucumber slices, to garnish

method

Using a sharp knife, cut the beef into $1/2$-inch/1-cm wide strips. Place them in a large, nonmetallic bowl.

To make the marinade, toast the sesame seeds in a heavy-bottom skillet over medium heat for 2–3 minutes, or until golden brown, shaking the skillet occasionally.

Place the seeds in a mortar with the garlic, ginger, and chili and, using a pestle, grind to a smooth paste. Add the soy sauce and curry paste and mix well.

Spoon the paste over the beef strips and toss to coat the meat evenly. Cover and let marinate in the refrigerator for at least 2–3 hours or overnight.

Heat a heavy-bottom skillet or ridged grill pan until very hot and brush with vegetable oil. Place the beef strips in the skillet and cook quickly, turning frequently, until lightly browned. Remove the skillet from the heat and spoon the beef into a pile on a hot serving dish.

Heat the sesame oil in a small skillet. Add the cashew nuts and quickly cook until golden. Add the scallion and stir-fry for 30 seconds. Sprinkle the mixture on top of the beef strips, then garnish with cucumber slices and serve immediately.

beef with onions & broccoli

ingredients

SERVES 4

2 tbsp. vegetable or peanut oil

2 tbsp. Thai green curry paste

2 6-oz/175 g sirloin steaks,
    sliced thinly

2 onions, sliced

6 scallions, chopped

2 shallots, chopped finely

8 oz/225 g broccoli, cut into
    florets

14 fl oz/400 ml/1¾ cups
    coconut milk

3 kaffir lime leaves, chopped
    coarsely

4 tbsp. chopped fresh cilantro

few Thai basil leaves

method

Heat the oil in a wok and stir-fry the curry paste for
1–2 minutes. Add the meat, in batches if necessary,
and stir-fry until starting to brown.

Add the onions, scallions, and shallots, and stir-fry for
2–3 minutes. Add the broccoli and stir-fry for 2–3 minutes.

Pour in the coconut milk, add the lime leaves, and bring
to a boil. Let simmer gently for 8–10 minutes, until the
meat is tender. Stir in the chopped cilantro and basil
leaves and serve immediately.

stir-fried beef with bean sprouts

ingredients

SERVES 4

1 bunch of scallions

2 tbsp. corn oil

1 garlic clove, crushed

1 tsp. finely chopped fresh
    gingerroot

1 lb 2 oz/500 g lean beef
    fillet, cut into thin strips

1 large red bell pepper,
    seeded and sliced

1 small fresh red chili, seeded
    and chopped

3 cups fresh bean sprouts

1 small lemongrass stem,
    finely chopped

2 tbsp. smooth peanut butter

4 tbsp. coconut milk

1 tbsp. rice vinegar or white
    wine vinegar

1 tbsp. soy sauce

1 tsp. brown sugar

9 oz/250 g medium egg
    noodles

salt and pepper

method

Thinly slice the scallions, reserving some slices to use
as a garnish.

Heat the oil in a skillet or preheated wok over high
heat. Add the scallions, garlic, and ginger and stir-fry
for 2–3 minutes to soften. Add the beef and continue
stir-frying for 4–5 minutes, or until evenly browned.

Add the bell pepper and stir-fry for an additional
3–4 minutes. Add the chili and bean sprouts and stir-fry
for 2 minutes. Mix the lemongrass, peanut butter, coconut
milk, vinegar, soy sauce, and sugar together in a bowl,
then stir into the skillet.

Meanwhile, cook the egg noodles in boiling salted water
for 4 minutes, or according to the package directions.
Drain and stir into the skillet, tossing to mix evenly.

Season to taste with salt and pepper. Sprinkle with the
reserved scallions and serve hot.

broiled beef salad

ingredients

SERVES 4

1³/₄ oz/50 g dried oyster
    mushrooms

1 lb 5 oz/600 g rump steak

1 red bell pepper, seeded and
    thinly sliced

scant ¹/₃ cup roasted cashew
    nuts

red and green lettuce leaves

fresh mint leaves, to garnish

dressing

2 tbsp. sesame oil

2 tbsp. Thai fish sauce

2 tbsp. sweet sherry

2 tbsp. oyster sauce

1 tbsp. lime juice

1 fresh red chili, seeded and
    finely chopped

method

Put the mushrooms in a heatproof bowl, cover with boiling water, and let stand for 20 minutes. Drain, then cut into slices.

Preheat the broiler to medium or heat a ridged grill pan. To make the dressing, place all the ingredients in a bowl and whisk to combine.

Cook the steak under the preheated grill or on the hot grill pan, turning once, for 5 minutes, or until browned on both sides but still rare in the center. Cook the steak longer if desired.

Slice the steak into thin strips and place in a bowl with the mushrooms, bell pepper, and nuts. Add the dressing and toss together.

Arrange the lettuce on a large serving platter and place the beef mixture on top. Garnish with mint leaves. Serve at room temperature.

red lamb curry

ingredients

SERVES 4

1 lb 2 oz/500 g lean boneless
   leg of lamb
2 tbsp. vegetable oil
1 large onion, sliced
2 garlic cloves, crushed
2 tbsp. Thai red curry paste
1/4 pint/150 ml/2/3 cup
   coconut milk
1 tbsp. brown sugar
1 large red bell pepper,
   seeded and thickly sliced
5 fl oz/150 ml/1/2 cup lamb or
   beef stock
1 tbsp. Thai fish sauce
2 tbsp. lime juice
generous 1 cup canned water
   chestnuts, drained
2 tbsp. chopped cilantro
2 tbsp. chopped fresh basil
salt and pepper
fresh basil leaves, to garnish
freshly cooked jasmine rice,
   to serve

method

Trim the meat and cut it into 1 1/4-inch/3-cm cubes. Heat
the oil in a large skillet or preheated wok over high heat.
Add the onion and garlic and stir-fry for 2–3 minutes to
soften. Add the meat and stir-fry the mixture quickly
until lightly browned.

Stir in the curry paste and cook for a few seconds, then
add the coconut milk and sugar and bring to a boil.
Reduce the heat and simmer for 15 minutes, stirring
occasionally.

Stir in the bell pepper, stock, fish sauce, and lime juice,
then cover and simmer for an additional 15 minutes, or
until the meat is tender.

Add the water chestnuts, cilantro, and basil and season
to taste with salt and pepper. Transfer to serving plates,
then garnish with basil leaves and serve with jasmine rice.

lamb with lime leaves

ingredients

SERVES 4

2 fresh red Thai chilies

2 tbsp. peanut oil

2 garlic cloves, crushed

4 shallots, chopped

2 lemongrass stems, sliced

6 fresh kaffir lime leaves

1 tbsp. tamarind paste

2 tbsp. palm sugar

1 lb/450 g lean boneless
    lamb (leg or loin fillet)

1/2 pint/300 ml/2 1/2 cups
    coconut milk

6 oz/175 g cherry tomatoes,
    halved

1 tbsp. chopped cilantro

freshly cooked Thai fragrant
    rice, to serve

method

Using a sharp knife, seed and very finely chop the chilies. Reserve until required.

Heat the oil in a large, preheated wok. Add the garlic, shallots, lemongrass, lime leaves, tamarind paste, sugar, and chilies to the wok and stir-fry for 2 minutes.

Using a sharp knife, cut the lamb into thin strips or cubes.

Add the lamb to the wok and stir-fry for 5 minutes, tossing well so that the lamb is evenly coated in the spice mixture.

Pour the coconut milk into the wok and bring to a boil. Reduce the heat and let simmer for 20 minutes.

Add the cherry tomatoes and chopped cilantro to the wok and simmer for 5 minutes. Transfer to serving plates and serve hot with fragrant rice.

stir-fried lamb with mint

ingredients

SERVES 4

generous ⅓ cup fresh mint
    leaves
2 tbsp. vegetable oil
2 garlic cloves, finely sliced
2 fresh red chilies, seeded
    and cut into thin strips
1 onion, thinly sliced
1½ tbsp. Madras curry paste
1 lb 2 oz/500 g lamb fillet,
    cut into thin strips
8 oz/225 g canned baby corn
    cobs, drained
4 scallions, finely chopped
1 tbsp. Thai fish sauce
freshly cooked rice, to serve

method

Coarsely shred the mint leaves and reserve until required.
Heat half the oil in a preheated wok or large skillet. Add
the garlic and chilies and cook until soft. Remove and
reserve. Add the onion and cook for 5 minutes, or until
soft. Remove and reserve.

Heat the remaining oil in the wok. Add the curry paste
and cook for 1 minute. Add the lamb, in batches if
necessary, and cook for 5–8 minutes, or until cooked
through and tender.

Return the onion to the wok with the baby corn cobs,
scallions, mint, and fish sauce. Cook until heated through.
Sprinkle the garlic and chilies over and serve with rice.

red curry pork
with bell peppers

ingredients

SERVES 4

2 tbsp. vegetable or peanut oil

1 onion, coarsely chopped

2 garlic cloves, chopped

1 lb/450 g pork fillet, sliced
   thickly

1 red bell pepper, seeded and
   cut into squares

6 oz/175 g mushrooms,
   quartered

2 tbsp. Thai red curry paste

4 oz/115 g block creamed
   coconut, chopped

1/2 pint/300 ml/1 1/4 cups pork
   or vegetable stock

2 tbsp. Thai soy sauce

4 tomatoes, peeled, seeded,
   and chopped

handful of fresh cilantro,
   chopped

boiled noodles or rice,
   to serve

method

Heat the oil in a wok or large skillet and sauté the onion
and garlic for 1–2 minutes, until they are softened but
not browned.

Add the pork slices and stir-fry for 2–3 minutes until
browned all over. Add the bell pepper, mushrooms, and
curry paste.

Dissolve the coconut in the hot stock and add to the wok
with the soy sauce. Bring to a boil and let simmer for
4–5 minutes until the liquid has reduced and thickened.

Add the tomatoes and cilantro and cook for 1–2 minutes
before serving with noodles or rice.

pad thai

ingredients

SERVES 4

8 oz/225 g thick rice-stick
    noodles

2 tbsp. vegetable or peanut oil

2 garlic cloves, chopped

2 fresh red chilies, seeded
    and chopped

6 oz/175 g pork fillet, sliced
    thinly

4 oz/115 g uncooked shrimp,
    shelled and chopped

8 fresh Chinese chives,
    chopped

2 tbsp. fish sauce

juice of 1 lime

2 tsp. jaggery or soft light
    brown sugar

2 eggs, beaten

4 oz/115 g/3/4 cup bean
    sprouts

4 tbsp. chopped fresh cilantro

4 oz/115 g/3/4 cup unsalted
    peanuts, chopped, plus
    extra to serve

crispy fried onions, to serve

method

Soak the noodles in warm water for 10 minutes, drain
well, and set aside.

Heat the oil in a wok and stir-fry the garlic, chilies, and
pork for 2–3 minutes. Add the shrimp and stir-fry for an
additional 2–3 minutes.

Add the chives and noodles, then cover and cook for
1–2 minutes. Add the fish sauce, lime juice, sugar,
and eggs. Cook, stirring and tossing constantly to mix
in the eggs.

Stir in the bean sprouts, cilantro, and peanuts, and
serve with small dishes of crispy fried onions and extra
chopped peanuts.

spicy fried ground pork

ingredients

SERVES 4

2 garlic cloves

3 shallots

1-inch/2.5-cm piece fresh
gingerroot

2 tbsp. corn oil

1 lb 2 oz/500 g ground lean
pork

2 tbsp. Thai fish sauce

1 tbsp. dark soy sauce

1 tbsp. Thai red curry paste

4 dried kaffir lime leaves,
crumbled

4 plum tomatoes, chopped

3 tbsp. chopped cilantro

salt and pepper

to garnish

cilantro sprigs

scallion tassels

freshly cooked fine egg
noodles, to serve

method

Finely chop the garlic, shallots, and ginger. Heat the oil
in a large skillet or preheated wok over medium heat.
Add the garlic, shallots, and ginger and stir-fry for
2 minutes. Stir in the pork and continue stir-frying until
golden brown.

Stir in the fish sauce, soy sauce, curry paste, and lime
leaves and stir-fry for an additional 1–2 minutes over
high heat.

Add the chopped tomatoes and cook for an additional
5–6 minutes, stirring occasionally. Stir in the chopped
cilantro and season to taste with salt and pepper.

Serve hot, spooned onto freshly cooked fine egg noodles,
garnished with cilantro sprigs and scallion tassels.

pork with vegetables

ingredients

SERVES 4

8 tbsp. vegetable or peanut oil

4 oz/115 g rice vermicelli
    noodles

4 belly pork strips, sliced
    thickly

1 red onion, sliced

2 garlic cloves, chopped

1-inch/2.5-cm piece fresh
    ginger, sliced thinly

1 large fresh red chili, seeded
    and chopped

4 oz/115 g baby corn, halved
    lengthwise

1 red bell pepper, seeded and
    sliced

6 oz/175 g broccoli, cut into
    florets

5$\frac{1}{2}$ oz/150 g jar black bean
    sauce

4 oz/115 g/$\frac{3}{4}$ cup bean
    sprouts

method

Heat the oil in a wok and cook the rice noodles, in batches, for 15–20 seconds, until they puff up. Remove with a slotted spoon, drain on paper towels, and set aside.

Pour off all but 2 tablespoons of the oil and stir-fry the pork, onion, garlic, ginger, and chili for 4–5 minutes, or until the meat has browned.

Add the corn, red bell pepper, and broccoli and stir-fry for 3–4 minutes, until the vegetables are just tender. Stir in the black bean sauce and bean sprouts, then cook for an additional 2–3 minutes. Serve immediately, topped with the crispy noodles.

pork with mixed green beans

ingredients

SERVES 4

2 tbsp. vegetable or peanut oil

2 shallots, chopped

8 oz/225 g pork fillet, sliced
thinly

1-inch/2.5-cm piece fresh
galangal, sliced thinly

2 garlic cloves, chopped

1/2 pint/300 ml/1 1/4 cups
chicken stock

4 tbsp. chili sauce

4 tbsp. crunchy peanut butter

4 oz/115 g fine green beans

4 oz/115 g/generous 1 cup
frozen fava beans

4 oz/115 g string beans,
sliced

crispy noodles, to serve

method

Heat the oil in a wok and stir-fry the shallots, pork, galangal, and garlic until lightly browned.

Add the chicken stock, chili sauce, and peanut butter, and stir until the peanut butter has melted. Add all the beans and let simmer for 3–4 minutes. Serve hot with crispy noodles.

pork with bell peppers

ingredients

SERVES 4

1 tbsp. vegetable or peanut oil

1 tbsp. chili oil

1 lb/450 g pork fillet, sliced
thinly

2 tbsp. green chili sauce

6 scallions, sliced

1-inch/2.5-cm piece fresh
ginger, sliced thinly

1 red bell pepper, seeded and
sliced

1 yellow bell pepper, seeded
and sliced

1 orange bell pepper, seeded
and sliced

1 tbsp. fish sauce

2 tbsp. Thai soy sauce

juice of 1/2 lime

4 tbsp. chopped fresh parsley

cooked flat rice noodles,
to serve

method

Heat both the oils in a wok. Add the pork, in batches,
and stir-fry until browned all over. Remove with a slotted
spoon and set aside.

Add the chili sauce, scallions, and ginger to the wok
and stir-fry for 1–2 minutes. Add the bell peppers and
stir–fry for 2–3 minutes.

Return the meat to the wok, stir well, and add the fish
sauce, soy sauce, and lime juice. Cook for an additional
1–2 minutes, then stir in the chopped parsley and serve
with flat rice noodles.

chicken & peanut curry

ingredients

SERVES 4

1 tbsp. vegetable or peanut oil

2 red onions, sliced

2 tbsp. Penang curry paste

14 fl oz/400 ml/1³⁄₄ cups
    coconut milk

¹⁄₄ cup/150 ml/²⁄₃ cup
    chicken stock

4 kaffir lime leaves, torn
    coarsely

1 lemongrass stalk, chopped
    finely

6 skinless, boneless chicken
    thighs, chopped

1 tbsp. fish sauce

2 tbsp. Thai soy sauce

1 tsp. jaggery or soft, light
    brown sugar

1³⁄₄ oz/50 g/¹⁄₂ cup unsalted
    peanuts, roasted and
    chopped, plus extra to
    garnish

6 oz/175 g fresh pineapple,
    chopped coarsely

6-inch/15-cm piece cucumber,
    peeled, seeded, and sliced
    thickly, plus extra to garnish

method

Heat the oil in a wok and stir-fry the onions for 1 minute.
Add the curry paste and stir-fry for 1–2 minutes.

Pour in the coconut milk and stock. Add the lime leaves
and lemongrass and let simmer for 1 minute. Add the
chicken and gradually bring to a boil. Let simmer for
8–10 minutes, until the chicken is tender.

Stir in the fish sauce, soy sauce, and sugar, and let
simmer for 1–2 minutes. Stir in the peanuts, pineapple,
and cucumber, and cook for 30 seconds. Serve
immediately, sprinkled with extra nuts and cucumber.

green chicken curry

ingredients

SERVES 4

1 tbsp. vegetable or peanut oil

1 onion, sliced

1 garlic clove, chopped finely

2–3 tbsp. Thai green curry
    paste

14 fl oz/400 ml/1³/₄ cups
    coconut milk

¹/₄ pint/150 ml/²/₃ cup
    chicken stock

4 kaffir lime leaves

4 skinless, boneless chicken
    breasts, cut into cubes

1 tbsp. fish sauce

2 tbsp. Thai soy sauce

grated rind and juice of ¹/₂ lime

1 tsp. jaggery or soft light
    brown sugar

4 tbsp. chopped fresh
    cilantro, to garnish

method

Heat the oil in a wok or large skillet and stir-fry the onion
and garlic for 1–2 minutes, until starting to soften. Add
the curry paste and stir-fry for 1–2 minutes.

Add the coconut milk, stock, and lime leaves, bring to a
boil and add the chicken. Reduce the heat and let simmer
gently for 15–20 minutes, until the chicken is tender.

Add the fish sauce, soy sauce, lime rind and juice, and
sugar. Cook for 2–3 minutes, until the sugar has dissolved.
Serve immediately, garnished with chopped cilantro.

chicken with yellow curry sauce

ingredients

SERVES 4

for the spice paste

6 tbsp. Thai yellow curry
    paste

1/4 pint/150 ml/2/3 cup plain
    yogurt

14 fl oz/400 ml/1 3/4 cups
    water

handful of fresh cilantro,
    chopped

handful of fresh Thai basil
    leaves, shredded

for the stir-fry

2 tbsp. vegetable or peanut oil

2 onions, cut into thin wedges

2 garlic cloves, chopped finely

2 skinless, boneless chicken
    breasts, cut into strips

6 oz/175 g baby corn, halved
    lengthwise

to garnish

chopped fresh cilantro

shredded fresh basil

method

To make the spice paste, stir-fry the yellow curry paste in a wok for 2–3 minutes, then stir in the yogurt, water, and herbs. Bring to a boil, then let simmer for 2–3 minutes.

Meanwhile, heat the oil in a wok and stir-fry the onions and garlic for 2–3 minutes. Add the chicken and corn and stir-fry for 3–4 minutes, until the meat and corn are tender.

Stir in the spice paste and bring to a boil. Let simmer for 2–3 minutes, until heated through. Serve immediately, garnished with extra herbs if desired.

ground chicken skewers

ingredients

SERVES 4

1 lb/450 g/2 cups ground
    chicken

1 onion, chopped finely

1 fresh red chili, seeded and
    chopped

2 tbsp. Thai red curry paste

1 tsp. jaggery or soft light
    brown sugar

1 tsp. ground coriander

1 tsp. ground cumin

1 egg white

8 lemongrass stalks

boiled rice with chopped
    scallion, to serve

method

Combine the chicken, onion, chili, curry paste, and sugar
in a bowl and stir well to make a thick paste. Stir in the
ground coriander, cumin, and egg white, and mix again.

Divide the mixture into 8 equal portions and squeeze
them around each of the lemongrass stalks. Arrange on
a grill pan and cook under high heat, turning frequently,
until browned and cooked through. Serve hot with the
rice with the scallion stirred through it.

gingered chicken kabobs

ingredients

SERVES 4

3 skinless, boneless chicken
    breasts, cut into cubes

juice of 1 lime

1-inch piece ginger, peeled
    and chopped

1 fresh red chili, seeded and
    sliced

2 tbsp. vegetable or peanut oil

1 onion, sliced

2 garlic cloves, chopped

1 eggplant, cut into chunks

2 zucchinis, cut into thick
    slices

1 red bell pepper, seeded and
    cut into squares

2 tbsp. Thai red curry paste

2 tbsp. Thai soy sauce

1 tsp. jaggery or soft light
    brown sugar

boiled rice, with chopped
    fresh cilantro, to serve

method

Put the chicken cubes in a shallow dish. Mix the lime, ginger, and chili together and pour over the chicken pieces. Stir gently to coat. Cover and let chill for at least 3 hours to marinate.

Thread the chicken pieces onto soaked wooden skewers and cook under a hot broiler for 3–4 minutes, turning often, until cooked through.

Meanwhile, heat the oil in a wok or large skillet and sauté the onion and garlic for 1–2 minutes, until softened but not browned. Add the eggplant, zucchini, and bell pepper and cook for 3–4 minutes, until cooked but still firm. Add the curry paste, soy sauce, and sugar, and cook for 1 minute.

Serve the vegetables and kabobs hot with boiled rice, stirred through with chopped cilantro.

spiced cilantro chicken

ingredients

SERVES 4

4 skinless, boneless chicken
    breasts
2 garlic cloves
1 fresh green chili, seeded
3/4-inch/2-cm piece fresh
    gingerroot
4 tbsp. chopped cilantro
finely grated rind of 1 lime
3 tbsp. lime juice
2 tbsp. light soy sauce
1 tbsp. superfine sugar
6 fl oz/170 ml/3/4 cup coconut
    milk

to garnish

finely chopped cilantro
cucumber slices
radish slices
1/2 fresh red chili, seeded and
    sliced into rings
freshly cooked rice, to serve

method

Using a sharp knife, cut 3 deep slashes into the skinned side of each chicken breast. Place the breasts in a single layer in a nonmetallic dish.

Place the garlic, chili, ginger, cilantro, lime rind and juice, soy sauce, sugar, and coconut milk in a food processor and process to a smooth paste.

Spread the paste over both sides of the chicken breasts, coating them evenly. Cover with plastic wrap and let marinate in the refrigerator for 1 hour.

Preheat the broiler to medium. Lift the chicken from the marinade, then drain off the excess and place on a broiler pan. Cook under the hot broiler for 12–15 minutes, or until thoroughly and evenly cooked.

Meanwhile, place the remaining marinade in a pan and bring to a boil. Reduce the heat and simmer for several minutes. Transfer the chicken breasts to serving plates. Garnish with chopped cilantro, cucumber slices, radish slices, and chili rings and serve with rice.

chicken with vegetables & cilantro rice

ingredients

SERVES 4

2 tbsp. vegetable or peanut oil

1 red onion, chopped

2 garlic cloves, chopped

1-inch/2.5-cm piece ginger, peeled and chopped

2 skinless, boneless chicken breasts, cut into strips

4 oz/115 g white mushrooms

14 oz/400 ml/1¾ cups canned coconut milk

2 oz/50 g sugar snap peas

2 tbsp. soy sauce

1 tbsp. fish sauce

for the rice

1 tbsp. vegetable or peanut oil

1 red onion, sliced

12 oz/350 g/3 cups rice, cooked and cooled

8 oz/250 g bok choy, torn into large pieces

handful of fresh cilantro, chopped

2 tbsp. Thai soy sauce

method

Heat the oil in a wok or large skillet and sauté the onion, garlic, and ginger together for 1–2 minutes.

Add the chicken and mushrooms and cook over high heat until browned. Add the coconut milk, sugar snap peas, and sauces, and bring to a boil. Let simmer gently for 4–5 minutes until tender.

Heat the oil for the rice in a separate wok or large skillet and cook the onion until softened but not browned. Add the cooked rice, bok choy, and fresh cilantro, and heat through gently until the leaves have wilted and the rice is hot. Sprinkle over the soy sauce and serve immediately with the chicken.

egg-fried rice with chicken

ingredients

SERVES 4

8 oz/225 g/generous 1 cup
    jasmine rice

3 skinless, boneless chicken
    breasts, cut into cubes

14 fl oz/400 ml/1¾ cups
    canned coconut milk

1¾ oz/50g block creamed
    coconut, chopped

2–3 cilantro roots, chopped

thinly pared rind of 1 lemon

1 fresh green chili, seeded
    and chopped

3 fresh Thai basil leaves

1 tbsp. fish sauce

1 tbsp. oil

3 eggs, beaten

for the garnish

fresh chives

sprigs fresh cilantro

method

Cook the rice in boiling water for 12–15 minutes, drain well, then let cool and chill overnight.

Put the chicken into a pan and cover with the coconut milk. Add the creamed coconut, cilantro roots, lemon rind, and chili, and bring to a boil. Let simmer for 8–10 minutes, until the chicken is tender. Remove from the heat. Stir in the basil and fish sauce.

Meanwhile, heat the oil in a wok and stir-fry the rice for 2–3 minutes. Pour in the eggs and stir until they have cooked and mixed with the rice. Line four small ovenproof bowls or ramekins with plastic wrap and pack with the rice. Turn out carefully onto serving plates and remove the plastic wrap. Garnish with long chives and sprigs of cilantro. Serve with the chicken.

ginger chicken with noodles

ingredients

SERVES 4

2 tbsp. vegetable or peanut oil

1 onion, sliced

2 garlic cloves, chopped finely

2-inch/5-cm piece fresh
   ginger, sliced thinly

2 carrots, sliced thinly

4 skinless, boneless chicken
   breasts, cut into cubes

1/2 pint/300 ml/1 1/4 cups
   chicken stock

4 tbsp. Thai soy sauce

8 oz/225 g canned bamboo
   shoots, drained and rinsed

2 3/4 oz/75 g flat rice noodles

for the garnish

4 scallions, chopped

4 tbsp. chopped fresh cilantro

method

Heat the oil in a wok and stir-fry the onion, garlic, ginger, and carrots for 1–2 minutes, until softened. Add the chicken and stir-fry for 3–4 minutes, until the chicken is cooked through and lightly browned.

Add the stock, soy sauce, and bamboo shoots, and gradually bring to a boil. Let simmer for 2–3 minutes. Meanwhile, soak the noodles in boiling water for 6–8 minutes. Drain well. Garnish with the scallions and cilantro and serve immediately, with the chicken stir-fry.

gingered chicken & vegetable salad

ingredients

SERVES 4

4 skinless, boneless chicken
    breasts
4 scallions, chopped
1-inch/2.5-cm piece ginger,
    chopped finely
2 garlic cloves, crushed
2 tbsp. vegetable or peanut oil

for the salad

1 tbsp. vegetable or peanut oil
1 onion, sliced
2 garlic cloves, chopped
4 oz/115 g baby corn, halved
4 oz/115 g snow peas, halved
    lengthwise
1 red bell pepper, seeded and
    sliced
3-inch/7.5-cm piece
    cucumber, peeled,
    seeded, and sliced
4 tbsp. Thai soy sauce
1 tbsp. soft light brown sugar
few Thai basil leaves
6 oz/175 g fine egg noodles

method

Cut the chicken into large cubes, each about 1 inch.
Mix the scallions, ginger, garlic, and oil together in a
shallow dish and add the chicken. Cover and let
marinate for at least 3 hours. Lift the meat out of the
marinade and set aside.

Heat the oil in a wok or large skillet and cook the onion
for 1–2 minutes before adding the rest of the vegetables
except the cucumber. Cook for 2–3 minutes, until just
tender. Add the cucumber, half the soy sauce, the
sugar, and the basil, and mix gently.

Soak the noodles for 2–3 minutes (check the package
instructions) or until tender, and drain well. Sprinkle the
remaining soy sauce over them and arrange on plates.
Top with the cooked vegetables.

Add a little more oil to the wok if necessary and cook the
chicken over fairly high heat until browned on all sides.
Arrange the chicken cubes on top of the salad and serve
hot or warm.

red chicken salad

ingredients

SERVES 4

4 boneless chicken breasts
2 tbsp. Thai red curry paste
2 tbsp. vegetable or peanut oil
1 head Napa cabbage,
    shredded
6 oz/175 g bok choy, torn into
    large pieces
1/2 savoy cabbage, shredded
2 shallots, chopped finely
2 garlic cloves, crushed
1 tbsp. rice wine vinegar
2 tbsp. sweet chili sauce
2 tbsp. Thai soy sauce

method

Slash the flesh of the chicken several times and rub the curry paste into each cut. Cover and let chill overnight.

Cook in a heavy-bottom pan over medium heat or on a grill pan for 5-6 minutes, turning once or twice, until cooked through. Keep warm.

Heat 1 tablespoon of the oil in a wok or large skillet and stir-fry the leaves, bok choy, and cabbage until just wilted. Add the remaining oil, shallots, and garlic, and stir-fry until just tender but not browned. Add the vinegar, chili sauce, and soy. Remove from the heat.

Arrange the leaves on 4 serving plates. Slice the chicken, arrange on the salad greens, and drizzle the hot dressing over. Serve immediately.

duck breasts with chili & lime

ingredients

SERVES 4

4 boneless duck breasts
2 garlic cloves, crushed
4 tsp. brown sugar
3 tbsp. lime juice
1 tbsp. soy sauce
1 tsp. chili sauce
1 tsp. vegetable oil
2 tbsp. plum jelly
5 fl oz/150 ml/1/2 cup chicken
  stock
salt and pepper

to serve

freshly cooked rice
crisp salad greens

method

Using a small, sharp knife, cut deep slashes in the skin of the duck to make a diamond pattern. Place the duck breasts in a wide, nonmetallic dish.

Mix the garlic, sugar, lime juice, soy sauce, and chili sauce together in a bowl, then spoon over the duck breasts, turning well to coat evenly. Cover and let marinate in the refrigerator for at least 3 hours or overnight.

Drain the duck, reserving the marinade. Heat a large, heavy-bottom skillet until very hot and brush with the oil. Add the duck breasts, skin-side down, and cook for 5 minutes, or until the skin is browned and crisp. Tip away the excess fat. Turn the duck breasts over.

Continue cooking on the other side for 2–3 minutes to brown. Add the reserved marinade, plum jelly, and stock and simmer for 2 minutes. Season to taste with salt and pepper. Transfer to individual serving plates, then spoon over the pan juices and serve hot with freshly cooked rice and crisp salad greens.

duck salad

ingredients

SERVES 4

4 boneless duck breasts,
　　skin on
1 lemongrass stalk, broken
　　into three and each cut in
　　half lengthwise
3 tbsp. vegetable or peanut oil
2 tbsp. sesame oil
1 tsp. fish sauce
1 fresh green chili, seeded
　　and chopped
2 tbsp. Thai red curry paste
1/2 fresh pineapple, peeled
　　and sliced
3-inch piece cucumber,
　　peeled, seeded, and sliced
3 tomatoes, cut into wedges
1 onion, sliced thinly

for the dressing

juice of 1 lemon
2 garlic cloves, crushed
1 tsp. jaggery or soft light
　　brown sugar
2 tbsp. vegetable or peanut oil

method

Unwrap the duck and let the skin dry out overnight in
the refrigerator.

The following day, slash the skin side 5 or 6 times. Mix
the lemongrass, 2 tablespoons of the vegetable oil, all the
sesame oil, fish sauce, chili, and curry paste together in
a shallow dish and place the duck breasts in the mixture.
Turn to coat and to rub the marinade into the meat. Let
chill for 2–3 hours.

Heat the remaining oil in a wok or large skillet and cook the
duck, skin-side down, over medium heat for 3–4 minutes
until the skin is browned and crisp and the meat cooked
most of the way through.

Turn the breasts over and cook until browned and the
meat is cooked to your liking.

Meanwhile, arrange the pineapple, cucumber, tomatoes,
and onions on a platter. Mix the dressing ingredients
together and pour over the top.

Lift the duck out of the wok and slice thickly. Arrange the
duck slices on top of the salad and serve while still hot.

for seafood fans

With Thailand's miles of coastline and many inland waterways, it is hardly surprising that the Thais are primarily a fish-eating nation. The warm tropical seas bring an abundance of fish and shellfish, while even the channels between the paddy fields are teeming with many types of fish.

In Thai coastal towns, there are rows of thatch-roofed beach kiosks selling fresh seafood from the warm Gulf waters – everything imaginable, from broiled or sautéed fish with ginger to shrimp in coconut and cilantro, is there to tempt both locals and visitors alike. Even in the heart of Bangkok city, the street markets are packed with fresh fish and seafood.

Like meat, fish and seafood are quickly transformed into delicious curries, stir-fries, and salads, and steaming in a traditional bamboo steamer is also a very popular method of cooking fish. Thick, meaty chunks of angler fish, cod, or salmon can be left for an hour or two in a refreshing chili and lime marinade, and hold their shape and texture perfectly as they are cooked. Creamy coconut milk features in many Thai dishes – it blends particularly well with the kick of Thai spices to create curry sauces with a delicate flavor that is perfect for fish.

mixed seafood curry

ingredients

SERVES 4

1 tbsp. vegetable or peanut oil

3 shallots, chopped finely

1-inch/2.5-cm piece fresh
    galangal, peeled and
    sliced thinly

2 garlic cloves, chopped finely

14 fl oz/400 ml/ 1¾ cups
    canned coconut milk

2 lemongrass stalks, snapped
    in half

4 tbsp. fish sauce

2 tbsp. chili sauce

8 oz/225 g uncooked jumbo
    shrimp, shelled

8 oz/225 g baby squid,
    cleaned and sliced thickly

8 oz/225 g skinned salmon
    fillet, cut into chunks

6 oz/175 g tuna steak, cut
    into chunks

8 oz/225 g fresh mussels,
    scrubbed and debearded

fresh Chinese chives, to garnish

boiled rice, to serve

method

Heat the oil in a large wok and stir-fry the shallots, galangal, and garlic for 1–2 minutes, until they start to soften. Add the coconut milk, lemongrass, fish sauce, and chili sauce. Bring to a boil, reduce the heat, and let simmer for 1–2 minutes.

Add the shrimp, squid, salmon, and tuna, and let simmer for 3–4 minutes, until the shrimp have turned pink and the fish is cooked.

Add the mussels and cover with a lid. Let simmer for 1–2 minutes, until they have opened. Discard any mussels that remain closed. Garnish with Chinese chives and serve immediately with rice.

fish curry

ingredients

SERVES 4

juice of 1 lime

4 tbsp. fish sauce

2 tbsp. Thai soy sauce

1 fresh red chili, seeded and
chopped

12 oz/350 g angler fish fillet,
cut into cubes

12 oz/350 g salmon fillets,
skinned and cut into
cubes

14 fl oz/400 ml/1¾ cups
coconut milk

3 kaffir lime leaves

1 tbsp. Thai red curry paste

1 lemongrass stalk (white part
only), chopped finely

8 oz/225 g/2 cups jasmine
rice, boiled

4 tbsp. chopped fresh cilantro

method

Combine the lime juice, half the fish sauce, and the soy
sauce in a shallow, nonmetallic dish. Add the chili and
the fish, stir to coat, cover with plastic wrap, and chill for
1–2 hours, or overnight.

Bring the coconut milk to a boil in a pan and add the
lime leaves, curry paste, the remaining fish sauce, and
the lemongrass. Let simmer gently for 10–15 minutes.

Add the fish and the marinade and let simmer for
4–5 minutes, until the fish is cooked. Serve hot with
boiled rice with chopped cilantro stirred through it.

fish curry with rice noodles

ingredients

SERVES 4

2 tbsp. vegetable or peanut oil

1 large onion, chopped

2 garlic cloves, chopped

3 oz/75g white mushrooms

8 oz/225 g angler fish, cut
into cubes, each about
1 inch/2.5 cm

8 oz/225 g salmon fillets, cut
into cubes, each about
1 inch/2.5 cm

8 oz/225 g cod, cut into
cubes, each about
1 inch/2.5 cm

2 tbsp. Thai red curry paste

14 oz/400 g/1¾ cups canned
coconut milk

handful of fresh cilantro,
chopped

1 tsp. soft light brown sugar

1 tsp. fish sauce

4 oz /115 g rice noodles

3 scallions, chopped

2 oz/50 g bean sprouts

few Thai basil leaves

method

Heat the oil in a wok or large skillet and gently sauté
the onion, garlic, and mushrooms until softened but
not browned.

Add the fish, curry paste, and coconut milk and bring
gently to a boil. Let simmer for 2–3 minutes before
adding half the the cilantro, the sugar, and fish sauce.
Keep warm.

Meanwhile, soak the noodles for 3–4 minutes (check
the package instructions) or until tender, and drain well
through a colander. Put the colander and noodles over a
pan of simmering water. Add the scallions, bean sprouts,
and most of the basil and steam on top of the noodles for
1–2 minutes or until just wilted.

Pile the noodles onto warmed serving plates and top
with the fish curry. Sprinkle the remaining cilantro and
basil over the top and serve immediately.

stir-fried rice noodles with marinated fish

ingredients

SERVES 4

1 lb/450 g angler fish or cod,
    cubed

8 oz/225 g salmon fillets,
    cubed

2 tbsp. vegetable or peanut oil

2 fresh green chilies, seeded
    and chopped

grated rind and juice of 1 lime

1 tbsp. fish sauce

4 oz/115 g wide rice noodles

2 tbsp. vegetable or peanut oil

2 shallots, sliced

2 garlic cloves, chopped finely

1 fresh red chili, seeded and
    chopped

2 tbsp. Thai soy sauce

2 tbsp. chili sauce

method

Place the fish in a shallow bowl. To make the marinade,
mix the oil, green chilies, lime juice and rind, and fish
sauce together and pour over the fish. Cover and chill
for 2 hours.

Put the noodles in a bowl and cover with boiling water.
Leave for 8–10 minutes (check the package instructions)
and drain well.

Heat the oil in a wok or large skillet and sauté the shallots,
garlic, and red chili until lightly browned. Add the soy
sauce and chili sauce. Add the fish and the marinade
to the wok and stir-fry gently for 2–3 minutes until
cooked through.

Add the drained noodles and stir gently. Sprinkle with
cilantro and serve immediately.

rice with seafood & squid

ingredients

SERVES 4

2 tbsp. vegetable or peanut oil

3 shallots, chopped finely

2 garlic cloves, chopped finely

8 oz/225 g/ generous 1 cup
    jasmine rice

1/2 pint/300 ml/1 1/4 cups fish
    stock

4 scallions, chopped

2 tbsp. Thai red curry paste

8 oz/225 g baby squid,
    cleaned and sliced thickly

8 oz/225 g white fish fillets,
    skinned and cut into
    cubes

8 oz/225 g salmon fillets,
    skinned and cut into
    cubes

4 tbsp. chopped fresh cilantro

method

Heat 1 tablespoon of the oil in a wok and stir-fry the shallots
and garlic for 2–3 minutes, until softened. Add the rice and
stir-fry for 2–3 minutes.

Add a ladleful of the stock and let simmer, adding more
stock as needed, for 12–15 minutes, until tender. Transfer
to a dish, let cool, and chill overnight.

Heat the remaining oil in a wok and stir-fry the scallions
and curry paste for 2–3 minutes. Add the squid and fish
and stir-fry gently to avoid breaking up the fish. Stir in
the rice and cilantro, heat through gently, and serve.

fish in coconut

ingredients

SERVES 4

2 tbsp. vegetable or peanut oil

6 scallions, chopped coarsely

1-inch/2.5 cm piece fresh
　　ginger, grated

2–3 tbsp. Thai red curry paste

14 fl oz/400 ml/1³/4 cups
　　coconut milk

¹/4 pint/150 ml/²/3 cup fish
　　stock

4 kaffir lime leaves

1 lemongrass stalk, halved

12 oz/350 g skinned white fish
　　fillets, cut into chunks

8 oz/225 g squid rings and
　　tentacles

8 oz/225 g large cooked
　　shelled shrimp

1 tbsp. fish sauce

2 tbsp. Thai soy sauce

4 tbsp. chopped fresh
　　Chinese chives

boiled jasmine rice with
　　chopped fresh cilantro,
　　to serve

method

Heat the oil in a wok or large skillet and stir-fry the scallions and ginger for 1–2 minutes. Add the curry paste and stir-fry for 1–2 minutes.

Add the coconut milk, fish stock, lime leaves, and lemongrass. Bring to a boil, then reduce the heat and let simmer for 1 minute.

Add the fish, squid, and shrimp, and let simmer for 2–3 minutes, until the fish is cooked. Add the fish and soy sauces and stir in the chives. Serve immediately with jasmine rice with fresh cilantro stirred through it.

spiced steamed fish

ingredients

SERVES 4–6

1-inch/2.5-cm piece fresh
  gingerroot, finely grated

1 lemongrass stem (base
  only), thinly sliced

6 fresh red chilies, seeded
  and coarsely chopped

1 small red onion, finely
  chopped

1 tbsp. Thai fish sauce

2 lb/900 g whole fish, cleaned

2 fresh kaffir lime leaves,
  thinly sliced

2 fresh basil sprigs

to serve

freshly cooked rice

cucumber, cut into thin sticks

method

Place the ginger, lemongrass, chilies, onion, and fish
sauce in a food processor. Process to a coarse paste,
adding a little water, if needed.

Cut 3–4 deep slits crosswise on each side of the fish.
Spread over the spice paste, rubbing it well into the slits.
Place the fish in a dish deep enough to hold the liquid
that collects during steaming. Sprinkle over the lime
leaves and basil.

Set up a steamer or place a rack into a wok or deep
pan. Bring about 2 inches/5 cm of water to a boil in the
steamer or wok.

Place the dish of fish into the steamer or on to the rack.
Reduce the heat to a simmer, then cover tightly and
steam the fish for 15–20 minutes, or until the fish is
cooked through. Serve with freshly cooked rice and
cucumber sticks.

steamed
yellow fish fillets

ingredients

SERVES 4

1 lb 2 oz/500 g firm fish fillets,
    such as red snapper, sole,
    or angler fish

1 red bird chili

1 small onion, chopped

3 garlic cloves, chopped

2 cilantro sprigs

1 tsp. coriander seeds

1/2 tsp. ground turmeric

1/2 tsp. pepper

1 tbsp. Thai fish sauce

2 tbsp. coconut milk

1 small egg, beaten

2 tbsp. rice flour

fresh red and green chili
    strips, to garnish

stir-fried vegetables, to serve

method

Using a sharp knife, remove any skin from the fish and
cut the fillets diagonally into 3/4-inch/2-cm wide strips.

Place the bird chili, onion, garlic, cilantro, and coriander
seeds in a mortar and, using a pestle, grind to make a
smooth paste.

Transfer the paste to a bowl and add the turmeric, pepper,
fish sauce, coconut milk, and beaten egg, stirring to mix
evenly. Spread the rice flour out on a large plate. Dip the
fish strips into the paste mixture, then into the rice flour
to coat lightly.

Bring the water in the bottom of a steamer to a boil, then
arrange the fish strips in the top of the steamer. Cover and
steam for 12–15 minutes, or until the fish is just firm.

Garnish the fish with the chili strips and serve immediately
with stir-fried vegetables.

pan-fried
spiced salmon

ingredients

SERVES 4

1-inch/2.5-cm piece fresh
gingerroot, grated

1 tsp. coriander seeds, crushed

$1/4$ tsp. chili powder

1 tbsp. lime juice

1 tsp. sesame oil

4 salmon fillet pieces with skin,
about $5^1/2$ oz/150 g each

2 tbsp. vegetable oil

cilantro leaves, to garnish

to serve

freshly cooked rice

stir-fried vegetables

method

Mix the ginger, crushed coriander, chili powder, lime juice, and sesame oil together in a bowl.

Place the salmon on a wide, nonmetallic plate or dish and spoon the mixture over the flesh side of the fillets, spreading it to coat each piece of salmon evenly.

Cover the dish with plastic wrap and let chill in the refrigerator for 30 minutes.

Heat a wide, heavy-bottom skillet or ridged grill pan with the vegetable oil over high heat. Place the salmon in the hot skillet, skin-side down, and cook for 4–5 minutes, without turning, until the salmon is crusty underneath and the flesh flakes easily.

Serve the salmon immediately, with freshly cooked rice, garnished with cilantro leaves, and stir-fried vegetables.

salmon with red curry in banana leaves

ingredients

SERVES 4

4 salmon steaks, about
6 oz/175 g each
2 banana leaves, halved
1 garlic clove, crushed
1 tsp. grated fresh gingerroot
1 tbsp. Thai red curry paste
1 tsp. brown sugar
1 tbsp. Thai fish sauce
2 tbsp. lime juice

to garnish

lime wedges
whole fresh red chilies
finely chopped fresh red chili

method

Preheat the oven to 425°F/220°C. Place a salmon steak in the center of each half banana leaf.

Mix the garlic, ginger, curry paste, sugar, and fish sauce together, then spread over the surface of the fish. Sprinkle with lime juice.

Carefully wrap the banana leaves around the fish, tucking in the sides as you go to make neat, compact pockets.

Place the pockets seam-side down on a baking sheet. Bake in the preheated oven for 15–20 minutes, or until the fish is cooked and the banana leaves are beginning to brown. Serve garnished with lime wedges, whole chilies, and finely chopped chili.

angler fish with lime and chili sauce

ingredients

SERVES 4

4 4-oz/115 g angler fish fillets

1 oz/25 g/$\frac{1}{4}$ cup rice flour or
cornstarch

6 tbsp. vegetable or peanut oil

4 garlic cloves, crushed

2 large fresh red chilies,
seeded and sliced

2 tsp. jaggery or soft light
brown sugar

juice of 2 limes

grated rind of 1 lime

boiled rice, to serve

method

Toss the fish in the flour, shaking off any excess. Heat the oil in a wok and cook the fish on all sides until browned and cooked through, taking care when turning not to break it up.

Lift the fish out of the wok and keep warm. Add the garlic and chilies and stir-fry for 1–2 minutes, until they have softened.

Add the sugar, the lime juice and rind, and 2–3 tablespoons of water and bring to a boil. Let simmer gently for 1–2 minutes, then spoon the mixture over the fish. Serve immediately with rice.

spiced tuna in sweet & sour sauce

ingredients

SERVES 4

4 fresh tuna steaks, about
    1 lb 2 oz/500 g in total
1/4 tsp. pepper
2 tbsp. peanut oil
1 onion, diced
1 small red bell pepper,
    seeded and cut into short
    thin sticks
1 garlic clove, crushed
1/2 cucumber, seeded and cut
    into short thin sticks
2 pineapple slices, diced
1 tsp. finely chopped fresh
    gingerroot
1 tbsp. brown sugar
1 tbsp. cornstarch
1 1/2 tbsp. lime juice
1 tbsp. Thai fish sauce
10 fl oz/300 ml/1 cup fish
    stock

to garnish

lime slices
cucumber slices

method

Sprinkle the tuna steaks with pepper on both sides. Heat a heavy-bottom skillet or ridged grill pan and brush with a little of the oil. Arrange the tuna steaks in the skillet and cook for 8 minutes, turning them over once.

Meanwhile, heat the remaining oil in a separate skillet. Add the onion, bell pepper, and garlic and cook gently for 3–4 minutes to soften.

Remove the skillet from the heat and stir in the cucumber, pineapple, ginger, and sugar.

Blend the cornstarch with the lime juice and fish sauce, then stir into the stock and add to the skillet. Stir over medium heat until boiling, then cook for 1–2 minutes, or until thickened and clear.

Spoon the sauce over the tuna and serve immediately, garnished with slices of lime and cucumber.

baked cod with a curry crust

ingredients

SERVES 4

1/2 tsp. sesame oil

4 cod fillet pieces, about
    5 1/2 oz/150 g each

6 oz/175 g/1 1/2 cups fresh
    white bread crumbs

2 tbsp. blanched almonds,
    chopped

2 tsp. Thai green curry paste

finely grated rind of 1/2 lime,
    plus extra thinly pared rind
    to garnish

salt and pepper

lime slices, to garnish

to serve

boiled new potatoes

mixed salad greens

method

Preheat the oven to 400°F/200°C. Brush the oil over the bottom of a wide, shallow ovenproof dish or pan, then arrange the cod pieces in a single layer.

Mix the bread crumbs, almonds, curry paste, and grated lime rind together in a bowl, stirring well to blend thoroughly and evenly. Season to taste with salt and pepper.

Carefully spoon the crumb mixture over the fish pieces, pressing lightly with your hand to hold it in place.

Bake the dish, uncovered, in the preheated oven for 35–40 minutes, or until the fish is cooked through and the crumb topping is golden brown.

Serve the dish hot, garnished with lime slices and rind and accompanied by boiled new potatoes and mixed salad greens.

sea bass & mango salad

ingredients

SERVES 2

2 small sea bass, cleaned
1 tbsp. Thai red curry paste
small handful of fresh
    cilantro, chopped
1/4 pint/150 ml/2/3 cup
    coconut milk
2 tbsp. sweet chili sauce
6-8 Thai basil leaves, chopped
1/2 tsp. fish sauce
1 tsp. rice wine vinegar
1 mango, seeded, peeled,
    and sliced
selection of mixed salad greens

method

Place the fish on a board. Mix the curry paste and cilantro together and stuff inside each fish cavity. Cover and let marinate for 1–2 hours.

Preheat the oven to 400°F/200°C. Place the fish in a roasting pan. Mix the coconut milk, chili sauce, basil, fish sauce, and vinegar, and pour over the fish. Arrange the mango slices in the pan as well. Cover with foil and cook for 15 minutes.

Remove the foil and cook uncovered for an additional 10–15 minutes until cooked.

Place the fish on 2 warmed serving plates, drizzle with the cooking sauces, and serve with the mixed salad greens.

stir-fried squid with hot black bean sauce

ingredients

SERVES 4

1 lb 10 oz/750 g squid, cleaned and tentacles discarded

1 large red bell pepper, seeded

scant 1 cup snow peas

1 head bok choy

3 tbsp. black bean sauce

1 tbsp. Thai fish sauce

1 tbsp. rice wine or dry sherry

1 tbsp. dark soy sauce

1 tsp. brown sugar

1 tsp. cornstarch

1 tbsp. water

1 tbsp. corn oil

1 tsp. sesame oil

1 small fresh red Thai chili, chopped

1 garlic clove, finely chopped

1 tsp. grated fresh gingerroot

2 scallions, chopped

method

Cut the squid body cavities into fourths lengthwise. Use the tip of a small, sharp knife to score a diamond pattern into the flesh, without cutting all the way through. Pat dry with paper towels.

Cut the bell pepper into long, thin slices. Cut the snow peas in half diagonally. Coarsely shred the bok choy.

Mix the black bean sauce, fish sauce, rice wine, soy sauce, and sugar together in a bowl. Blend the cornstarch with the water and stir into the other sauce ingredients. Reserve until required.

Heat the oils in a preheated wok. Add the chili, garlic, ginger, and scallions and stir-fry for 1 minute. Add the bell pepper slices and stir-fry for 2 minutes.

Add the squid and stir-fry over high heat for an additional 1 minute. Stir in the snow peas and bok choy and stir for an additional 1 minute, or until wilted.

Stir in the sauce ingredients and cook, stirring constantly, for 2 minutes, or until the sauce thickens and clears. Serve immediately.

squid & red bell peppers

ingredients

SERVES 4

for the spice paste

2 tbsp. vegetable or peanut oil

1 tbsp. chili oil with shrimp

2 shallots, chopped

2–3 large fresh red chilies,
seeded and chopped

2 tbsp. ground coriander

2 tbsp. ground cumin

1-inch/2.5-cm piece fresh
ginger, chopped

1 tbsp. finely chopped
lemongrass

3–4 cilantro roots, chopped

1 tsp. salt

1 tsp. soft light brown sugar

for the stir-fry

2 red bell peppers, seeded
and diced

1/4 pint/150 ml/2/3 cup plain
yogurt

1 lb 10 oz/750 g squid,
cleaned and sliced

juice of 1 lime

4 oz/115 g block creamed
coconut, chopped

1/4 pint/150 ml/2/3 cup hot
water

method

Put all the ingredients for the spice paste into a food processor and process until chopped finely.

Scrape the spice paste into a wok and stir-fry gently for 3–4 minutes. Add the red bell peppers and stir-fry for 1–2 minutes.

Add the yogurt and bring to a boil. Add the squid and let simmer for 2–3 minutes, then stir in the lime juice, coconut, and water. Let simmer for an additional 1–2 minutes, until the coconut dissolves. Serve immediately.

spicy scallops with lime & chili

ingredients

SERVES 4

16 large scallops, shelled
1 tbsp. butter
1 tbsp. vegetable oil
1 tsp. crushed garlic
1 tsp. grated fresh gingerroot
1 bunch of scallions,
    finely sliced
finely grated rind of 1 lime
1 small fresh red chili, seeded
    and very finely chopped
3 tbsp. lime juice
lime wedges, to garnish
freshly cooked rice, to serve

method

Using a sharp knife, trim the scallops to remove any black intestine, then wash and pat dry with paper towels. Separate the corals from the white parts, then slice each white part in half horizontally, making 2 circles.

Heat the butter and oil in a skillet or preheated wok. Add the garlic and ginger and stir-fry for 1 minute without browning. Add the scallions and stir-fry for an additional 1 minute.

Add the scallops and continue stir-frying over high heat for 4–5 minutes. Stir in the lime rind, chili, and lime juice and cook for an additional 1 minute.

Transfer the scallops to serving plates, then spoon over the pan juices and garnish with lime wedges. Serve hot with freshly cooked rice.

curried noodles with shrimp & straw mushrooms

ingredients

SERVES 4

1 tbsp. vegetable or peanut oil

3 shallots, chopped

1 fresh red chili, seeded and chopped

1 tbsp. Thai red curry paste

1 lemongrass stalk (white part only), chopped finely

8 oz/225 g cooked shelled shrimp

14 oz/400 g canned straw mushrooms, drained

2 tbsp. fish sauce

2 tbsp. Thai soy sauce

8 oz/225 g fresh egg noodles

fresh cilantro, chopped, to garnish

method

Heat the oil in a wok and stir-fry the shallots and chili for 2–3 minutes. Add the curry paste and lemongrass and stir-fry for 2–3 minutes.

Add the shrimp, mushrooms, fish sauce, and soy sauce, and stir well to mix.

Meanwhile, cook the noodles in boiling water for 3–4 minutes, drain, and transfer to warmed plates. Top with the shrimp curry, sprinkle the cilantro over, and serve immediately.

shrimp & pineapple curry

ingredients

SERVES 4

1/2 fresh pineapple
14 fl oz/400 ml/1 3/4 cups
    coconut cream
2 tbsp. Thai red curry paste
2 tbsp. fish sauce
2 tsp. sugar
12 oz/350 g raw jumbo shrimp
2 tbsp. chopped cilantro
steamed jasmine rice, to serve

method

Peel the pineapple and chop the flesh. Heat the coconut cream, pineapple, curry paste, fish sauce, and sugar until almost boiling.

Shell and devein the shrimp. Add the shrimp and chopped cilantro to the pan and simmer for 3 minutes, or until the shrimp are cooked – they are cooked when they have turned a bright pink color.

Serve the shrimp with steamed jasmine rice.

noodles with shrimp & green bell peppers

ingredients

SERVES 4

9 oz/250 g rice noodles

1 tbsp. vegetable oil

2 garlic cloves, crushed

1 fresh red chili, seeded and
thinly sliced

1 green bell pepper, seeded
and thinly sliced

6 scallions, coarsely chopped

2 tsp. cornstarch

2 tbsp. oyster sauce

1 tbsp. Thai fish sauce

1 tsp. sugar

10 fl oz/300 ml/1 cup
chicken stock

9 oz/250 g small cooked
shrimp, shelled

method

Prepare the noodles according to the package directions. Drain, then rinse under cold water and drain again.

Heat the oil in a preheated wok. Add the garlic, chili, bell pepper, and scallions. Cook for 1 minute, then transfer to a plate and reserve.

Blend the cornstarch with a little water and add to the wok with the oyster sauce, fish sauce, sugar, and stock. Stir over medium heat until the mixture boils and thickens.

Return the bell pepper and scallion mixture to the wok with the shrimp and noodles. Cook, stirring, for 2 minutes, or until heated through. Transfer to a heated serving bowl and serve immediately.

shrimp with noodles

ingredients

SERVES 4

1 lb/450 g uncooked jumbo
    shrimp

1 tbsp. vegetable or peanut oil

3 shallots, chopped finely

2 garlic cloves, chopped finely

1-inch piece fresh ginger,
    sliced thinly

14 fl oz/400 ml/1¾ cups
    canned coconut milk

1 tbsp. Thai green curry paste

3–4 fresh Thai basil leaves

1 tsp. jaggery or soft light
    brown sugar

8 oz/225 g flat rice noodles

2 tsp. sesame oil

2 tbsp. sesame seeds, toasted

sprigs fresh Thai basil,
    to garnish

method

Remove and discard the heads and shell the shrimp.
Cut a slit along the back of each and remove and
discard the dark vein.

Heat the oil in a wok and stir-fry the shallots, garlic, and
ginger for 2–3 minutes. Add the coconut milk and curry
paste and let simmer for 2–3 minutes.

Add the shrimp, basil leaves, and sugar, and cook until
the shrimp turn pink.

Meanwhile, cook the noodles in boiling water according
to the package instructions, then drain well. Stir in the
sesame oil and seeds, garnish with the sprigs of basil,
and serve immediately with the shrimp.

shrimp with coconut rice

ingredients

SERVES 4

4 oz/115 g/1 cup dried Chinese
    mushrooms

2 tbsp. vegetable or peanut oil

6 scallions, chopped

2 oz/55 g/scant $^1/_2$ cup dry
    unsweetened coconut

1 fresh green chili, seeded
    and chopped

8 oz/225 g/generous 1 cup
    jasmine rice

$^1/_4$ pint/150 ml/$^2/_3$ cup fish
    stock

14 fl oz/400 ml/1$^3/_4$ cups
    coconut milk

12 oz/350 g cooked shelled
    shrimp

6 sprigs fresh Thai basil

method

Place the mushrooms in a small bowl, cover with hot water, and set aside to soak for 30 minutes. Drain, then cut off and discard the stalks and slice the caps.

Heat 1 tablespoon of the oil in a wok and stir-fry the scallions, coconut, and chili for 2–3 minutes, until lightly browned. Add the mushrooms and stir-fry for 3-4 minutes.

Add the rice and stir-fry for 2-3 minutes, then add the stock and bring to a boil. Reduce the heat and add the coconut milk. Let simmer for 10–15 minutes, until the rice is tender. Stir in the shrimp and basil, heat through, and serve.

shrimp with scallions & straw mushrooms

ingredients

SERVES 4

2 tbsp. vegetable or peanut oil

bunch of scallions, chopped

2 garlic cloves, chopped finely

6 oz/175 g block creamed
    coconut, chopped
    coarsely

2 tbsp. Thai red curry paste

3/4 pint/450 ml/ scant 2 cups
    fish stock

2 tbsp. fish sauce

2 tbsp. Thai soy sauce

6 sprigs fresh Thai basil

14 oz/400 g canned straw
    mushrooms, drained

12 oz/350 g large cooked
    shelled shrimp

boiled jasmine rice, to serve

method

Heat the oil in a wok and stir-fry the scallions and garlic for 2–3 minutes. Add the creamed coconut, red curry paste, and fish stock, and heat gently until the coconut has dissolved.

Stir in the fish sauce and soy sauce, then add the basil, mushrooms, and shrimp. Gradually bring to a boil and serve immediately with jasmine rice.

made with
vegetables

Thai food is ideal for both strict vegetarians and for those who enjoy their vegetables crisply cooked and bursting with goodness and flavor. A wonderful range of vegetables is grown in Thailand, from eggplant and scallions to a variety of vibrant greens including bok choy and beans.

Protein in vegetarian dishes is provided by tofu (a nutritious cholesterol-free soybean curd with a bland taste, which readily absorbs flavorings) and nuts such as cashews, making for an exceptionally healthy diet that is low in saturated fats and sodium. As with meat and fish dishes, rice and noodles are a big feature of vegetable-based meals. Noodles come in a variety of shapes and sizes; some are made, rather like pasta, from wheat flour, eggs, and water, but noodles made from rice or from ground mung beans have a lighter texture and are ideal for those on a gluten-free diet.

Thai vegetable dishes are undoubtedly perfect for the health-conscious, but they are also delicious, quick and easy to make, and form an essential part of an authentic Thai meal, where they will join a selection of meat- and fish-based dishes. Note that, for strict vegetarians, you should use vegetable rather than chicken stock where relevant, and omit ingredients such as shrimp paste and fish sauce.

eggplant & bean curry

ingredients

SERVES 4

2 tbsp. vegetable or peanut oil

1 onion, chopped

2 garlic cloves, crushed

2 fresh red chilies, seeded and chopped

1 tbsp. Thai red curry paste

1 large eggplant, cut into chunks

4 oz/115 g pea or small eggplants

generous 1 cup baby fava beans

4 oz/115 g fine green beans

1/2 pint/300 ml/1 1/4 cups vegetable stock

2 oz/55 g block creamed coconut, chopped

3 tbsp. Thai soy sauce

1 tsp. jaggery or soft light brown sugar

3 kaffir lime leaves, torn coarsely

4 tbsp. chopped fresh cilantro

method

Heat the oil in a wok or large skillet and sauté the onion, garlic, and chilies for 1–2 minutes. Stir in the curry paste and cook for 1–2 minutes.

Add the eggplants and cook for 3–4 minutes, until starting to soften. (You may need to add a little more oil as eggplants soak it up quickly.) Add all the beans and stir-fry for 2 minutes.

Pour in the stock and add the creamed coconut, soy sauce, sugar, and lime leaves. Bring gently to a boil and cook until the coconut has dissolved. Stir in the cilantro and serve hot.

eggplant & mushroom stuffed omelet

ingredients

SERVES 4

3 tbsp. vegetable oil

1 garlic clove, finely chopped

1 small onion, finely chopped

1 small eggplant, diced

1/2 small green bell pepper, seeded and chopped

1 large dried shiitake mushroom, soaked, drained, and sliced

1 tomato, diced

1 tbsp. light soy sauce

1/2 tsp. sugar

1/4 tsp. pepper

2 large eggs

to garnish

salad greens

tomato wedges

cucumber slices

dipping sauce, to serve

method

Heat half the oil in a large skillet. Add the garlic and cook over high heat for 30 seconds. Add the onion and the eggplant and continue to stir-fry until golden.

Add the bell pepper and stir-fry for an additional 1 minute to soften. Stir in the mushroom, tomato, soy sauce, sugar, and pepper. Remove from the skillet and keep hot.

Beat the eggs together lightly. Heat the remaining oil in a clean skillet, swirling to coat a wide area. Pour in the egg and swirl to set around the skillet.

When the egg is set, spoon the filling into the center. Fold in the sides of the omelet to form a square package.

Slide the omelet carefully on to a warmed dish and garnish with salad greens, tomato wedges, and cucumber slices. Serve with a dipping sauce.

stuffed eggplants

ingredients

SERVES 4

8 small eggplants

2 tbsp. vegetable or peanut oil

4 shallots, chopped finely

2 garlic cloves, crushed

2 fresh red chilies, seeded
    and chopped

1 zucchini, chopped coarsely

4 oz/115 g block creamed
    coconut, chopped

few Thai basil leaves, chopped

small handful of fresh
    cilantro, chopped

4 tbsp. Thai soy sauce

to serve

rice with chopped scallions

sweet chili sauce

method

Preheat the oven to 400°F/200°C. Put the eggplants in a roasting pan and cook for 8–10 minutes, until just softened. Cut in half and scoop out the flesh, reserving the shells.

Heat the oil in a wok or large skillet and sauté the shallots, garlic, and chili for 2–3 minutes before adding the zucchinis and eggplant flesh. Add the creamed coconut, the herbs, and soy sauce, and let simmer for 3–4 minutes.

Divide the mixture between the eggplant shells. Return to the oven for 5–10 minutes, until hot and serve immediately with rice and sweet chili sauce.

tofu & green vegetable curry

ingredients

SERVES 4

vegetable oil, for deep-frying

8 oz/225 g firm tofu, cubed

2 tbsp. vegetable or peanut oil

1 tbsp. chili oil

2 fresh green chilies, seeded
    and sliced

2 garlic cloves, crushed

6 scallions, sliced

2 medium zucchinis, cut into
    sticks

1/2 cucumber, peeled,
    seeded, and sliced

1 green bell pepper, seeded
    and sliced

1 small head broccoli, cut
    into florets

2 oz/55 g fine green beans,
    halved

2 oz/55 g/ scant 1/2 cup
    frozen peas, thawed

1/2 pint/300 ml/1 1/4 cups
    vegetable stock

2 oz/55 g block creamed
    coconut, chopped

2 tbsp. Thai soy sauce

1 tsp. soft light brown sugar

4 tbsp. chopped fresh parsley

method

Heat the oil for deep-frying in a skillet and carefully lower
in the tofu cubes, in batches, and cook for 2–3 minutes,
until golden brown. Remove with a slotted spoon and
drain on paper towels.

Heat the other oils in a wok and stir-fry the chilies, garlic,
and scallions for 2–3 minutes. Add the zucchinis, cucumber,
green bell pepper, broccoli, and green beans, and stir-fry for
an additional 2–3 minutes.

Add the peas, stock, coconut, soy sauce, and sugar. Cover
and let simmer for 2–3 minutes, until all the vegetables are
tender and the coconut has dissolved.

Stir in the tofu and serve immediately, sprinkled with the
chopped fresh parsley.

rice noodles with mushrooms & tofu

ingredients

SERVES 4

8 oz/225 g rice stick noodles

2 tbsp. vegetable oil

1 garlic clove, finely chopped

3/4-inch/2-cm piece fresh gingerroot, finely chopped

4 shallots, thinly sliced

1 1/4 cups sliced shiitake mushrooms

3 1/2 oz/100 g firm tofu (drained weight), cut into 5⁄8-inch/ 1.5-cm dice shapes

2 tbsp. light soy sauce

1 tbsp. rice wine or dry sherry

1 tbsp. Thai fish sauce

1 tbsp. smooth peanut butter

1 tsp. chili sauce

2 tbsp. toasted peanuts, chopped

shredded fresh basil leaves

method

Place the rice noodles in a bowl, then cover with hot water and let soak for 15 minutes, or according to the package directions. Drain well.

Heat the oil in a large skillet. Add the garlic, ginger, and shallots and stir-fry for 1–2 minutes, or until softened and lightly browned.

Add the mushrooms and stir-fry for an additional 2–3 minutes. Stir in the tofu and toss gently to brown lightly.

Mix the soy sauce, rice wine, fish sauce, peanut butter, and chili sauce together in a small bowl, then stir into the skillet.

Stir in the rice noodles and toss to coat evenly in the sauce. Sprinkle with peanuts and shredded basil leaves and serve hot.

vegetables with tofu & spinach

ingredients

SERVES 4

vegetable or peanut oil, for deep-frying

8 oz/225 g firm tofu, drained and cut into cubes

2 tbsp. vegetable or peanut oil

2 onions, chopped

2 garlic cloves, chopped

1 fresh red chili, seeded and sliced

3 celery stalks, sliced diagonally

8 oz/225 g mushrooms, sliced thickly

4 oz/115 g baby corn, cut in half

1 red bell pepper, seeded and cut into strips

3 tbsp. Thai red curry paste

14 fl oz/400 ml/1¾ cups coconut milk

1 tsp. soft light brown sugar

2 tbsp. Thai soy sauce

8 oz/225 g/5 cups baby spinach leaves

method

Heat the oil in a skillet and deep-fry the tofu cubes, in batches, for 4–5 minutes, until crisp and browned. Remove with a slotted spoon and drain on paper towels.

Heat 2 tablespoons of the oil in a wok or skillet and stir-fry the onions, garlic, and chili for 1–2 minutes, until they start to soften. Add the celery, mushrooms, corn, and red bell pepper, and stir-fry for 3–4 minutes, until they soften.

Stir in the curry paste and coconut milk and gradually bring to a boil. Add the sugar and soy sauce and then the spinach. Cook, stirring constantly, until the spinach has wilted. Serve immediately, topped with the tofu.

cauliflower & beans with cashews

ingredients

SERVES 4

1 tbsp. vegetable or peanut oil

1 tbsp. chili oil

1 onion, chopped

2 garlic cloves, chopped

2 tbsp. Thai red curry paste

1 small cauliflower, cut into
    florets

6 oz/175 g yard-long beans,
    cut into 3-inch lengths

$1/4$ pint/150 ml/$2/3$ cup
    vegetable stock

2 tbsp. Thai soy sauce

$1^3/4$ oz/50 g/scant $1/3$ cup
    toasted cashews, to
    garnish

method

Heat both the oils in a wok and stir-fry the onion and garlic until softened. Add the curry paste and stir-fry for 1–2 minutes.

Add the cauliflower and beans and stir-fry for 3–4 minutes, until softened. Pour in the stock and soy sauce and let simmer for 1–2 minutes. Serve immediately, garnished with the cashews.

spiced cashew nut curry

ingredients

SERVES 4

8³/₄ oz/250 g/1²/₃ cups
    unsalted cashew nuts
1 tsp. coriander seeds
1 tsp. cumin seeds
2 cardamom pods, crushed
1 tbsp. corn oil
1 onion, finely sliced
1 garlic clove, crushed
1 small fresh green chili,
    seeded and chopped
1 cinnamon stick
¹/₂ tsp. ground turmeric
4 tbsp. coconut cream
¹/₂ pint/300 ml/1¹/₄ cups hot
    vegetable stock
3 dried kaffir lime leaves,
    crumbled
cilantro leaves, to garnish
freshly cooked jasmine rice,
    to serve

method

Place the cashew nuts in a bowl, then cover with cold water and let soak overnight. Drain thoroughly. Crush the seeds and cardamom pods in a mortar using a pestle.

Heat the oil in a large skillet. Add the onion and garlic and stir-fry for 2–3 minutes to soften but not brown. Add the chili, crushed spices, cinnamon stick, and turmeric and stir-fry for an additional 1 minute.

Add the coconut cream and the hot stock to the skillet. Bring to a boil, then add the cashew nuts and lime leaves.

Cover the skillet, then reduce the heat and simmer for 20 minutes. Serve hot with jasmine rice garnished with cilantro leaves.

zucchini & cashew curry

ingredients

SERVES 4

2 tbsp. vegetable or peanut oil

6 scallions, chopped

2 garlic cloves, chopped

2 fresh green chilies, seeded and chopped

1 lb/450 g zucchinis, cut into thick slices

4 oz/115 g shiitake mushrooms, halved

2 oz/50 g/$\frac{1}{2}$ cup bean sprouts

3 oz/75 g/$\frac{1}{2}$ cup cashews, toasted or dry-fried

few Chinese chives, chopped

4 tbsp. Thai soy sauce

1 tsp. fish sauce

rice or noodles, to serve

method

Heat the oil in a wok or large skillet and sauté the onions, garlic, and chilies for 1–2 minutes, until softened but not browned.

Add the zucchinis and mushrooms to the wok and cook for 2–3 minutes until tender.

Add the bean sprouts, nuts, chives, and both sauces and stir-fry for 1–2 minutes.

Serve hot with rice or noodles.

sweet-and-sour vegetables with cashews

ingredients

SERVES 4

1 tbsp. vegetable or peanut oil

1 tsp. chili oil

2 onions, sliced

2 carrots, sliced thinly

2 zucchinis, sliced thinly

4 oz/115 g broccoli, cut into
   florets

4 oz/115 g white mushrooms,
   sliced

4 oz/115 g small bok choy,
   halved

2 tbsp. jaggery or soft light
   brown sugar

2 tbsp. Thai soy sauce

1 tbsp. rice vinegar

3 oz/75 g/ $^{1}/_{2}$ cup cashews

method

Heat both the oils in a wok or skillet and stir-fry the onions for 1–2 minutes, until they start to soften.

Add the carrots, zucchinis, and broccoli, and stir-fry for 2–3 minutes. Add the mushrooms, bok choy, sugar, soy sauce, and rice vinegar, and stir-fry for 1-2 minutes.

Meanwhile, dry-fry or toast the cashews. Sprinkle the cashews over the stir-fry and serve immediately.

vegetable & coconut curry

ingredients

SERVES 4

2 lb. 4 oz/1 kg mixed
vegetables

1 onion, coarsely chopped

3 garlic cloves, thinly sliced

1-inch/2.5-cm piece fresh
gingerroot, thinly sliced

2 fresh green chilies, seeded
and finely chopped

1 tbsp. vegetable oil

1 tsp. ground turmeric

1 tsp. ground coriander

1 tsp. ground cumin

7 oz/200 g creamed coconut

1 pint/600 ml/2¹/₂ cups
boiling water

salt and pepper

2 tbsp. chopped cilantro,
to garnish

freshly cooked rice, to serve

method

Cut the mixed vegetables into chunks. Place the onion, garlic, ginger, and chilies in a food processor and process until almost smooth.

Heat the oil in a large, heavy-bottom skillet. Add the onion mixture and cook for 5 minutes.

Add the turmeric, coriander, and cumin and cook for 3–4 minutes, stirring. Add the mixed vegetables and stir to coat in the spice paste.

Mix the creamed coconut and boiling water together in a pitcher. Stir until the coconut has dissolved. Add the coconut milk to the vegetables, then cover and simmer for 30–40 minutes, or until the vegetables are tender.

Season to taste with salt and pepper, then garnish with the chopped cilantro and serve with rice.

mixed vegetables with quick-fried basil

ingredients

SERVES 4

2 tbsp. vegetable or peanut oil

2 garlic cloves, chopped

1 onion, sliced

4 oz/115 g baby corn, cut in
half diagonally

1/2 cucumber, peeled, halved,
seeded, and sliced

8 oz canned water chestnuts,
drained and rinsed

2 oz/60 g snow peas, trimmed

4 oz/115 g shiitake
mushrooms

1 red bell pepper, seeded and
sliced thinly

1 tbsp. soft light brown sugar

2 tbsp. Thai soy sauce

1 tbsp. fish sauce

1 tbsp. rice vinegar

boiled rice, to serve

for the quick-fried basil

vegetable or peanut oil, for
cooking

8-12 sprigs fresh Thai basil

method

Heat the oil in a wok and stir-fry the garlic and onion for
1-2 minutes. Add the corn, cucumber, water chestnuts,
snow peas, mushrooms, and red bell pepper, and stir-fry
for 2–3 minutes, until starting to soften.

Add the sugar, soy sauce, fish sauce, and vinegar, and
gradually bring to a boil. Let simmer for 1–2 minutes.

Meanwhile, heat the oil for the basil in a wok or skillet, and
when hot, add the basil sprigs. Cook for 20–30 seconds,
until crisp. Remove with a slotted spoon and drain
thoroughly on paper towels.

Garnish the vegetable stir-fry with the crispy basil and
serve immediately, with the boiled rice.

asian vegetables with yellow bean sauce

ingredients

SERVES 4

1 eggplant

salt

2 tbsp. vegetable oil

3 garlic cloves, crushed

4 scallions, chopped

1 small red bell pepper,
    seeded and thinly sliced

4 baby corn cobs, halved
    lengthwise

scant 1 cup snow peas

7 oz/200 g green bok choy,
    coarsely shredded

14^1/$_2$ oz/425 g canned straw
    mushrooms, drained

^{3}/$_4$ cup bean sprouts

2 tbsp. rice wine or dry sherry

2 tbsp. yellow bean sauce

2 tbsp. dark soy sauce

1 tsp. chili sauce

1 tsp. sugar

5 fl oz/150 ml/^{1}/$_2$ cup
    vegetable stock

1 tsp. cornstarch

2 tsp. water

method

Cut the eggplant into 2-inch/5-cm long thin sticks. Place in a colander, then sprinkle with salt and let stand for 30 minutes. Rinse in cold water and dry with paper towels.

Heat the oil in a skillet or preheated wok. Add the garlic, scallions, and bell pepper and stir-fry over high heat for 1 minute. Stir in the eggplant pieces and stir-fry for an additional 1 minute, or until softened.

Stir in the corn cobs and snow peas and stir-fry for 1 minute. Add the bok choy, mushrooms, and bean sprouts and stir-fry for 30 seconds.

Mix the rice wine, yellow bean sauce, soy sauce, chili sauce, and sugar together in a bowl, then add to the skillet with the stock. Bring to a boil, stirring constantly.

Slowly blend the cornstarch with the water to form a smooth paste, then stir quickly into the skillet and cook for an additional 1 minute. Serve immediately.

egg-fried rice with vegetables & crispy onions

ingredients

SERVES 4

4 tbsp. vegetable or peanut oil

2 garlic cloves, chopped finely

2 fresh red chilies, seeded
   and chopped

4 oz/115 g mushrooms,
   sliced

2 oz/50 g snow peas, halved

2 oz/50 g baby corn, halved

3 tbsp. Thai soy sauce

1 tbsp. jaggery or soft light
   brown sugar

few Thai basil leaves

12 oz/350 g/3 cups rice,
   cooked and cooled

2 eggs, beaten

2 onions, sliced

method

Heat half the oil in a wok or large skillet and sauté the
garlic and chilies for 2–3 minutes.

Add the mushrooms, snow peas, and corn, and stir-fry
for 2–3 minutes before adding the soy sauce, sugar, and
basil. Stir in the rice.

Push the mixture to one side of the wok and add the
eggs to the bottom. Stir until lightly set before combining
into the rice mixture.

Heat the remaining oil in another skillet and sauté the
onions until crispy and brown. Serve the rice topped
with the onions.

potato & spinach yellow curry

ingredients

SERVES 4

2 garlic cloves, finely chopped

1¼-inch/3-cm piece fresh galangal, finely chopped

1 lemongrass stem, finely chopped

1 tsp. coriander seeds

3 tbsp. vegetable oil

2 tsp. Thai red curry paste

½ tsp. ground turmeric

6 fl oz/170 ml/generous ¾ cup coconut milk

9 oz/250 g potatoes, cut into ¾-inch/2-cm cubes

5 fl oz/300 ml/scant ½ cup vegetable stock

7 oz/200 g fresh young spinach leaves

1 small onion, thinly sliced

method

Place the garlic, galangal, lemongrass, and coriander seeds in a mortar and, using a pestle, grind to make a smooth paste.

Heat 2 tablespoons of the oil in a skillet or preheated wok. Stir in the garlic paste mixture and stir-fry for 30 seconds. Stir in the curry paste and turmeric, then add the coconut milk and bring to a boil.

Add the potatoes and stock. Return to a boil, then reduce the heat and simmer, uncovered, for 10–12 minutes, or until the potatoes are almost tender.

Stir in the spinach and simmer until the leaves are wilted.

Meanwhile, heat the remaining oil in a separate skillet. Add the onion and cook until crisp and golden brown.

Place the crispy fried onions on top of the curry just before serving.

carrot &
pumpkin curry

ingredients

SERVES 4

1/4 pint/150 ml/2/3 cup
  vegetable stock

1-inch/2.5-cm piece fresh
  galangal, sliced

2 garlic cloves, chopped

1 lemongrass stalk (white part
  only), chopped finely

2 fresh red chilies, seeded
  and chopped

4 carrots, peeled and cut into
  chunks

8 oz/225 g pumpkin, peeled,
  seeded, and cut into cubes

2 tbsp. vegetable or peanut oil

2 shallots, chopped finely

3 tbsp. Thai yellow curry
  paste

14 fl oz/400 ml/1 3/4 cups
  coconut milk

4–6 sprigs fresh Thai basil

1 oz/25 g/1/8 cup toasted
  pumpkin seeds, to garnish

method

Pour the stock into a large pan and bring to a boil. Add
the galangal, half the garlic, the lemongrass, and chilies,
and let simmer for 5 minutes. Add the carrots and
pumpkin and let simmer for 5–6 minutes, until tender.

Meanwhile, heat the oil in a wok or skillet and stir-fry the
shallots and the remaining garlic for 2–3 minutes. Add
the curry paste and stir-fry for 1–2 minutes.

Stir the shallot mixture into the pan and add the coconut
milk and basil. Let simmer for 2–3 minutes. Serve hot,
sprinkled with the toasted pumpkin seeds.

stir-fried ginger mushrooms

ingredients

SERVES 4

2 tbsp. vegetable oil

3 garlic cloves, crushed

1 tbsp. Thai red curry paste

1/2 tsp. ground turmeric

15 oz/425 g canned straw
mushrooms, drained and
halved

3/4-inch/2-cm piece fresh
gingerroot, finely shredded

5 fl oz/300 ml/scant 1/2 cup
coconut milk

1 1/2 oz/40 g dried shiitake
mushrooms, soaked,
drained, and sliced

1 tbsp. lemon juice

1 tbsp. light soy sauce

2 tsp. sugar

1/2 tsp. salt

8 cherry tomatoes, halved

7 oz/200 g firm tofu, diced

cilantro leaves, for sprinkling

scallion curls, to garnish

Thai fragrant rice, to serve

method

Heat the oil in a preheated wok or large skillet. Add the garlic and cook for 1 minute, stirring. Stir in the curry paste and turmeric and cook for an additional 30 seconds.

Stir in the straw mushrooms and ginger and stir-fry for 2 minutes. Stir in the coconut milk and bring to a boil.

Stir in the shiitake mushrooms, lemon juice, soy sauce, sugar, and salt and heat thoroughly. Add the tomatoes and tofu and toss gently to heat through.

Sprinkle the cilantro over the mixture and serve hot with freshly cooked fragrant rice garnished with scallion curls.

julienne
vegetable salad

ingredients

SERVES 4

4 tbsp. vegetable or peanut oil

8 oz/225 g tofu with herbs,
    cubed

1 red onion, sliced

4 scallions, cut into 2-inch
    lengths

1 garlic clove, chopped

2 carrots, cut into short,
    thin sticks

4 oz/115 g fine green beans,
    trimmed

1 yellow bell pepper, seeded
    and cut into strips

4 oz/115 g broccoli florets

1 large zucchini, cut into
    short, thin sticks

1/2 cup bean sprouts

2 tbsp. Thai red curry paste

4 tbsp. Thai soy sauce

1 tbsp. rice wine vinegar

1 tsp. soft light brown sugar

few Thai basil leaves

12 oz/350 g rice vermicelli
    noodles

method

Heat the oil in a wok or large skillet and cook the tofu
cubes for 3–4 minutes, until browned on all sides. Lift
out of the oil and drain on paper towels.

Add the onions, garlic, and carrots to the hot oil and cook
for 1–2 minutes before adding the rest of the vegetables,
except for the bean sprouts. Stir-fry for 2–3 minutes.
Add the bean sprouts, then stir in the curry paste, soy,
vinegar, sugar, and basil leaves. Cook for 30 seconds.

Soak the noodles in boiling water or stock for 2–3 minutes
(check the package instructions) or until tender, and
drain well.

Pile the vegetables onto the noodles, and serve topped
with the tofu cubes. Garnish with extra basil if desired.

to finish

This chapter on desserts, rather like the appetizers chapter, is something of a departure from authentic Thai culinary tradition, because the Thai people usually finish their meals with nothing more than a basket of their fabulous tropical fruits, such as mangoes, guavas, pineapples, and litchis. There are no dairy products in Thailand, so the familiar Western desserts and "comfort puddings," rich in cream or chocolate, simply do not exist.

The recipes here, therefore, are a combination of dishes using the wonderful, colorful fruits and exotic flavorings of Thailand, such as the Tropical Fruit in Lemongrass Syrup illustrated here, to a few definite "cheats" like the Banana & Coconut Ice Cream and the Creamy Mango Brûlée, a marvellous fusion of East and West in one small ramekin.

Coconuts are grown in Thailand and their flesh and "milk" are used extensively in cooking, forming almost as important a part of the diet as rice. Coconut products are readily available in cans and cartons, but you can use a fresh coconut – if you can get into it. The best way is to hold the coconut over a bowl to catch the milk and, using a hammer, tap around the centre of the shell until it cracks in half.

roasted spicy pineapple

ingredients

SERVES 4

1 pineapple

1 mango, peeled, seeded, and sliced

2 oz/55 g butter

4 tbsp. corn syrup

1–2 tsp. cinnamon

1 tsp. freshly grated nutmeg

4 tbsp. soft brown sugar

2 passion fruit

1/4 pint/150 ml/2/3 cup sour cream

finely grated rind of 1 orange

method

Preheat the oven to 400°F/200°C. Use a sharp knife to cut off the top, base, and skin of the pineapple, then cut into fourths. Remove the central core and cut the flesh into large cubes. Place them in a roasting pan with the mango.

Place the butter, syrup, cinnamon, nutmeg, and sugar in a small pan and heat gently, stirring constantly, until melted. Pour the mixture over the fruit. Roast for 20–30 minutes, until the fruit is browned.

Halve the passion fruit and scoop out the seeds. Spoon over the roasted fruit. Mix the sour cream and orange rind together and serve with the fruit.

pineapple with cardamom & lime

ingredients

SERVES 4

1 pineapple

2 cardamom pods

thinly pared lime rind

4 tbsp. water

1 tbsp. brown sugar

3 tbsp. lime juice

to decorate

fresh mint sprigs

whipped cream

method

Cut the top and base from the pineapple, then cut away the peel and remove the "eyes" from the flesh. Cut into fourths and remove the core. Slice the pineapple lengthwise and place in a large serving dish.

Crush the cardamom pods in a mortar using a pestle and place in a pan with the lime rind and water. Bring the mixture to a boil, then reduce the heat and simmer for 30 seconds.

Remove the pan from the heat and add the sugar, then cover with a lid and let infuse for 5 minutes.

Stir in the sugar to dissolve, add the lime juice, then strain the syrup over the pineapple. Cover and let chill in the refrigerator for 30 minutes.

When ready to serve, decorate with mint sprigs and a spoonful of whipped cream.

pineapple & lime sherbet

ingredients

SERVES 4

8 oz/225 g/generous 1 cup
    superfine sugar
1 pint/600 ml/2¹/₂ cups water
grated rind and juice of 2 limes
1 small pineapple, peeled,
    quartered, and chopped
sweet cookies, to serve

method

Put the sugar and water into a pan and heat gently, stirring until the sugar has dissolved. Bring to a boil and let simmer for 10 minutes.

Stir in the grated rind and half the lime juice. Remove from the heat and let cool.

Put the pineapple in a blender or food processor and process until smooth. Add to the cold syrup with the remaining lime juice. Pour into a freezerproof container and freeze until crystals have formed around the edge.

Turn out the sherbet into a bowl. Beat well with a fork to break up the crystals. Return to the freezer and chill overnight. Serve in scoops with sweet cookies.

grilled bananas

ingredients

SERVES 4

2 oz/55 g block creamed
    coconut, chopped
$1/4$ pint/150 ml/$2/3$ cup
    heavy cream
4 bananas
juice and rind of 1 lime
1 tbsp. vegetable or peanut oil
$1^3/4$ oz/50 g/scant $1/2$ cup dry
    unsweetened coconut

method

Put the creamed coconut and cream in a small pan and heat gently until the coconut has dissolved. Remove from the heat and set aside to cool for 10 minutes, then whisk until thick but floppy.

Peel the bananas and toss in the lime juice and rind. Lightly oil a preheated grill pan and cook the bananas, turning once, for 2–3 minutes, until soft and browned.

Toast the dry unsweetened coconut on a piece of foil under a broiler until lightly browned. Serve the bananas with the coconut cream, sprinkled with the toasted coconut.

bananas in coconut milk

ingredients

SERVES 4

4 large bananas

12 fl oz/350 ml/1 1/2 cups
   coconut milk

2 tbsp. superfine sugar

pinch of salt

1 tsp. orange flower water

1 tbsp. shredded fresh mint

2 tbsp. cooked mung beans

fresh mint sprigs, to decorate

method

Peel the bananas and cut them into short chunks. Place in a large pan with the coconut milk, sugar, and salt. Heat gently until boiling and simmer for 1 minute. Remove the pan from the heat.

Sprinkle the orange flower water over the banana mixture. Stir in the mint and spoon into a serving dish.

Place the mung beans in a heavy-bottom skillet and cook over high heat until they turn crisp and golden, shaking the skillet occasionally. Let the beans cool slightly, then crush lightly in a mortar using a pestle.

Sprinkle the toasted beans over the bananas and serve warm or cold, decorated with mint sprigs.

banana-stuffed crêpes

ingredients

SERVES 4

8 oz/225 g/1½ cups all-
   purpose flour

2 tbsp. soft light brown sugar

2 eggs

¾ pint/450 ml/generous
   1¾ cups milk

grated rind and juice of 1 lemon

2 oz/55 g butter

3 bananas

4 tbsp. corn syrup

method

Combine the flour and sugar and beat in the eggs and half the milk. Beat together until smooth. Gradually add the remaining milk, stirring constantly to make a smooth batter. Stir in the lemon rind.

Melt a little butter in an 8-inch skillet and pour in one-quarter of the batter. Tilt the skillet to coat the bottom and cook for 1–2 minutes, until set. Flip the crêpe over and cook the second side. Slide out of the skillet and keep warm. Repeat to make 3 more crêpes.

Slice the bananas and toss in the lemon juice. Pour the syrup over them and toss together. Fold each crêpe in half and then in half again and fill the center with the banana mixture. Serve warm.

banana & coconut ice cream

ingredients

SERVES 6–8

3 oz/85 g block creamed
    coconut, chopped

1 pint/600 ml/2¹/₂ cups heavy
    cream

8 oz/225 g/1 cup
    confectioners' sugar

2 bananas

1 tsp. lemon juice

fresh fruit, to serve

method

Put the creamed coconut in a small bowl. Add just enough boiling water to cover and stir until the coconut is dissolved. Let cool.

Whip the cream with the confectioners' sugar until thick but still floppy. Mash the bananas with the lemon juice and whisk gently into the cream, along with the cold coconut.

Transfer to a freezerproof container and freeze overnight. Serve in scoops with fresh fruit.

mango &
lime sherbet

ingredients

SERVES 4

4 oz/115 g/1/2 cup superfine
    sugar
1/4 pint/150 ml/ 1/2 cup water
finely grated rind of 3 limes
2 tbsp. coconut cream
2 large ripe mangoes
1/4 pint/150 ml/scant 2/3 cup
    lime juice
curls of fresh coconut,
    toasted, to decorate

method

Place the sugar, water, and lime rind in a small pan and
heat gently, stirring constantly, until the sugar dissolves.
Boil rapidly for 2 minutes to reduce slightly, then remove
the pan from the heat and strain into a heatproof bowl or
pitcher. Stir in the coconut cream and let cool.

Halve the mangoes, then remove the pits and peel thinly.
Chop the flesh coarsely and place in a food processor with
the lime juice. Process to a smooth purée and transfer to a
small bowl.

Pour the cooled syrup into the mango purée, mixing
evenly. Tip into a large, freezerproof container and freeze
for 1 hour, or until slushy in texture. Alternatively, use an
ice cream machine.

Remove the container from the freezer and beat with an
electric mixer to break up the ice crystals. Refreeze for
an additional 1 hour, then remove from the freezer and
beat the contents again until smooth.

Cover the container, then return to the freezer and leave
until firm. To serve, remove from the freezer and let stand
at room temperature for 15 minutes before scooping into
individual glass dishes. Sprinkle with toasted coconut
to decorate.

creamy mango brûlée

ingredients

SERVES 4

2 mangoes

9 oz/250 g/generous 1 cup
    mascarpone cheese

7 fl oz/200 ml/generous
    ³/4 cup strained plain
    yogurt

1 tsp. ground ginger

grated rind and juice of 1 lime

2 tbsp. soft light brown sugar

8 tbsp. raw brown sugar

method

Slice the mangoes on either side of the seed. Discard the seed and peel the fruit. Slice and then chop the fruit. Divide it between 4 ramekins.

Beat the mascarpone cheese with the yogurt. Fold in the ginger, lime rind and juice, and soft brown sugar. Divide the mixture between the ramekins and level off the tops. Chill for 2 hours.

Sprinkle 2 tablespoons of raw brown sugar over the top of each dish, covering the creamy mixture. Place under a hot broiler for 2–3 minutes, until melted and browned. Let cool, then chill until needed. This dessert should be eaten on the day made.

mangoes in lime syrup

ingredients

SERVES 4

2 large ripe mangoes
1 lime
1 lemongrass stem, chopped
3 tbsp. superfine sugar

method

Halve the mangoes, then remove the pits and peel off the skins.

Slice the flesh into long, thin slices and carefully arrange them in a wide serving dish.

Remove a few shreds of the rind from the lime for decoration, then cut the lime in half and squeeze out the juice.

Place the lime juice in a small pan with the lemongrass and sugar. Heat gently without boiling until the sugar is completely dissolved. Remove the pan from the heat and let cool completely.

Strain the cooled syrup into a small pitcher and pour evenly over the mango slices.

Sprinkle with the lime rind strips. Cover and let chill in the refrigerator before serving. Serve chilled.

litchi & ginger sherbet

ingredients

SERVES 4

1 lb 12 oz/800 g canned
    litchis in syrup
finely grated rind of 1 lime
2 tbsp. lime juice
3 tbsp. preserved ginger syrup
2 egg whites

to decorate

carambola slices
slivers of preserved ginger

method

Drain the litchis, reserving the syrup. Place the litchis in a food processor or blender with the lime rind, juice, and preserved ginger syrup and process until completely smooth. Transfer to a large bowl.

Mix the purée thoroughly with the reserved litchi syrup, then pour into a large, freezerproof container and freeze for 1–1½ hours, or until slushy in texture. Alternatively, use an ice cream machine.

Remove from the freezer and whisk to break up the ice crystals. Whisk the egg whites in a clean, dry bowl until stiff, then quickly and lightly fold into the ice mixture.

Return to the freezer and leave until firm. Serve the sherbet in scoops, with slices of carambola and preserved ginger to decorate.

mixed fruit salad

ingredients

SERVES 4

1 papaya, halved, peeled,
   and seeded

2 bananas, sliced thickly

1 small pineapple, peeled,
   halved, cored, and sliced

12 litchis, peeled if fresh

1 small melon, seeded and
   cut into thin wedges

2 oranges

grated rind and juice of 1 lime

2 tbsp. superfine sugar

method

Arrange the papaya, bananas, pineapple, litchis, and melon on a serving platter. Cut off the rind and pith from the oranges. Cut the orange slices out from between the membranes and add to the fruit platter. Grate a small quantity of the discarded orange rind and add to the platter.

Combine the lime rind, juice, and sugar. Pour over the salad and serve.

tropical fruit in lemongrass syrup

ingredients

SERVES 4

1 honeydew melon

1 small pineapple

1 papaya

14 oz/400 g litchis, pitted

3 passion fruit

lemongrass syrup

3 oz/90 g/³/₄ cup superfine
    sugar

¹/₄ pint/150 ml/²/₃ cup water

2 lemongrass stems, bruised

2 fresh kaffir lime leaves

juice of 1 lime

to decorate

1 tbsp. grated lime rind

small handful of fresh mint
    leaves

method

To make the syrup, place all the ingredients in a pan. Heat gently until the sugar has dissolved. Bring to a boil and cook, uncovered, for 5 minutes. Let stand overnight.

Cut the melon in half, then remove the seeds and scoop out the flesh with a melon baller. Place in a bowl. Peel the pineapple, cut into fourths lengthwise, and remove the core. Cut into cubes and add to the melon. Peel the papaya, then remove the seeds, cut the flesh into cubes, and add to the other fruits.

Add the litchis. Cut the passion fruit in half and scoop the pulp and seeds into the bowl of fruits. Stir to mix, then transfer to a serving bowl. Remove the lemongrass and lime leaves from the syrup and pour over the fruits. Decorate with the lime rind and mint leaves and serve.

spicy rice pudding

ingredients

SERVES 4

14 fl oz/400 ml/1³/4 cups
    canned coconut milk

¹/4 pint/150 ml/²/3 cup milk

2 oz/55 g/generous ¹/4 cup
    light soft brown sugar

2 oz/55 g/generous ¹/4 cup
    short-grain rice

2 tsp. allspice

1 oz butter

1 tsp. ground cinnamon

method

Put the coconut milk and milk in a pan and heat gently.
Add the sugar and stir until it has dissolved.

Add the rice and spice and gradually bring to a boil. Let
simmer gently, stirring frequently, for 45–60 minutes,
until thickened.

Stir in the butter, and once it has melted, serve immediately,
sprinkled with cinnamon.

coconut cake with lime & ginger syrup

ingredients

SERVES 4

2 large eggs, separated

pinch of salt

2 oz/55 g/$^{1}/_{2}$ cup superfine sugar

5 tbsp. butter, melted and cooled

5 tbsp. coconut milk

4 oz/115 g/1 cup self-rising flour

$^{1}/_{2}$ tsp. baking powder

3 tbsp. dry unsweetened coconut

4 tbsp. preserved ginger syrup

3 tbsp. lime juice

to decorate

3 pieces preserved ginger

curls of fresh coconut

finely grated lime rind

method

Cut an 11-inch/28-cm circle of parchment paper and press into a 7-inch/18-cm steamer basket to line it.

Whisk the egg whites with the salt in a clean, dry bowl until stiff. Gradually whisk in the sugar, 1 tablespoon at a time, whisking hard after each addition until the mixture forms stiff peaks.

Whisk in the yolks, then quickly stir in the butter and coconut milk. Sift the flour and baking powder over the mixture, then fold in lightly and evenly with a large metal spoon. Fold in the coconut.

Spoon the mixture into the lined steamer basket and tuck the spare paper over the top. Place the basket over boiling water, then cover and steam for 30 minutes.

Transfer the cake to a plate, remove the paper, and let cool slightly. Mix the ginger syrup and lime juice together and spoon over the cake. Cut into squares and decorate with pieces of preserved ginger, curls of coconut, and lime rind.